Flipside

A MEMOIR

BY

LEEANN JORDAN

ACKNOWLEDGMENTS

I would like to thank so many people!

My sister, L. Lynn Adams, also the published author of the devotional book, Take Another Step With Jesus. She is named 'Jetta' in my story. The two of us share a bond so deep, full of so many memories – I leaned on her hard throughout my journey, and she was there for me every step of the way. She's my closest confidante, my accountability partner, my greatest encourager, and one of the most defining Christian mentors anyone could ever have.

My parents: They opened their home to me and took me in, caring for me in every single way with compassion and unconditional love. They've prayed for me every day of my life, and still do. They are my first go-to for advice and Biblical direction. My parents, along with Lynn, drove me to all kinds of appointments and experienced every change alongside me. Their home is always a safe refuge for me.

My family as a whole: Especially my oldest sister, Laurie (Jada), My brother, Jim, and his wife, Ruby (Les and Gemma), and their son, Isaac (Ian). My son, Joel

(Jude), my daughter, Jordan (Jamie), and her husband, Hadyn (Henry). Every single one has been there for me, carrying my many needs in frequent, heartfelt, effective prayer. The constancy of knowing they're in my corner is a tremendous gift.

Patricia B., my best friend. She's named 'Dana' in my story. She showed a friendship depth that I've never experienced before or since. She understands. She REALLY gets it. All of it. She's still dealing with the awful aftermath of cancer herself, but goes out of her way to support me at every turn.

My other friends, especially Michael (Matt), his mom, Sherry (Shelly), and his sister, Lacole (Linea), who always bring with them fun and laughter and the steadiness of life going on.

Every doctor, surgeon, nurse, aide, anesthesiologist, specialist, tech, therapist, and assistant who took such great, compassionate, personalized care of me.

My church family and Ladies' Bible Study group, who supported me and prayed for me through the whole thing.

Contents

PROLOGUE

I've written this book as my own story. I've changed all the names, including my own, just for the fun of it. I've always loved the name Jessie and most names that start with J, as you'll no doubt see. I've also been deliberately vague about places. Again, just because I could.

This story is my own life journey. It is not meant to elevate me to a pedestal status, find fault with anyone else's personal journey, or mirror anyone else's journey. It's very personal and very descriptive. In some ways, it's also very different from any other story I've heard.

I've delved into some of my life history so that my readers could better understand the depth and breadth of my 'nurse' mindset. It will hopefully become somewhat apparent how very weird and unsettling it is for a nurse to become a patient. I could medically understand all that was being done, and had even performed almost all the nursing duties involved, but I had to wrap my head around the fact of it all being done to me. Maybe this is not something non-medical people deal with. For me, it was BIG. And it still is.

I hope you appreciate the frank rawness of this book. I've made no attempt to soften the rough edges. I've also made no attempt at 'political correctness'. I make no apology for either. This is me – who I really am, imperfections and all. The struggles, the new realities all along the way, and my/our reactions to them, as well as lessons learned from them, are, again, very personal.

Rather uniquely, I had the immense privilege of receiving almost all my medical care from people I had worked with and trusted, most of whom I'm still friends with today. It was an experience I'm sure is rare and not enjoyed by all patients. Every single one of them showed me compassion and treated me from their hearts. I owe them a debt I can never repay.

Please enjoy!

WHAT'S WRONG WITH ME?????

Why am I so short of breath? I'm panting after just a few steps! I wanna put this nasal cannula of oxygen on myself instead of on the patient! And why am I so exhausted? I slept really well the past few nights, but my whole body feels like lead. I love this job, and it's so much easier physically than almost every job I've ever had, so why do I constantly feel like I'm struggling to keep up? And the anxiety! I feel so out of control. It doesn't make sense!

And that's how it all began...

CHAPTER ONE

COVID-19 screwed up the world. It changed everything from how people shop to how they work to how they have meetings and classes. It became a far-reaching fear and a weirdly secluding force.

It also meant that I had to (got to?) postpone my yearly physical. So turning 50 came and went as no big deal. My life was set in a pattern I'd chosen, and I was actually enjoying it.

I'm a nurse. I love being a nurse. I love getting to connect with all different kinds of people. I love the challenge of keeping up with and learning all the new developments in medicine and medical equipment. I love getting to be actively involved in saving lives. I love seeing the lightbulb come on in people as I explain and translate medical-ese into words they can understand. I love teaching people how to take care of their specific problems. I love getting to watch the progress of healing taking place. I love the relief on the faces of both patients and their loved ones, as the medicine I give relieves pain or nausea. I love sharing in the tears of joy as a precious new life comes into the world. I love the privilege of being a comforting presence when a patient or family receives bad news or the patient takes their final breaths.

As a friend of mine in EMS put it, "I get to do a job I love, use my skills and knowledge to help the community I love, and often take care of people I know and love." Yeah, that was me to a T. I couldn't describe myself better. I loved it all.

Sure, there were rough days. It wasn't all smiles. Sure, there were things I'd rather not have to do, and times I was so overwhelmed and exhausted I thought I wanted to give up. But still, I loved it.

The medical world is a jumbled maze to the uninitiated. As a medical professional, the choices of work environment seem almost limitless. Often, what you start out to do, the career you decide on in college is not the only path you end up taking.

I started out at age 16. I needed to get a job and didn't really want to. Obviously, I had no developed skills in anything yet, and honestly, I felt I didn't really have any strong abilities. There was no strong pull in any direction at all. But my oldest sister was a nurse, and that seemed interesting, so I applied at a local nursing home. They were offering a nurse aide training course and employment upon successful completion of the brief training. It seemed like an easy way to get a job, so I was happy when they accepted my application.

And then the actual training started...

Do you have any idea how HARD a nurse aide works?! That job is extremely physically demanding! An aide spends almost every minute of their shift on their feet. Most of that time is spent in manual labor. And let me tell you, it's no easy thing to keep a whole hall full of people clean, fed, dressed well, toileted on time, and happy.

I've heard people jokingly (or not) say a nurse aide in a nursing home is nothing but a 'butt wiper'. And yes, they do wipe people's butts – often and repeatedly. Not going to lie: some parts of the job can be really gross. But what's the alternative? Let them sit there in their own filth? Absolutely unacceptable! Someone has to be willing to do the hard things. Someone has to care enough. Someone has to have the guts, the intestinal fortitude to humble themselves for the sake of others who can't help themselves.

Giving someone a shower is challenging too. Especially if the patient (usually called a 'resident') is resisting the process. Imagine trying to shower someone who is hitting, kicking, biting, yelling, and trying to get away from you. A good nurse aide becomes very adept at handling all kinds of unexpected behaviors and still getting the job done well.

Or turn it around, and imagine not knowing where you are; nothing is familiar. You can't see very well, you can't hear very well, you can't walk very well. Then, suddenly, this stranger shows up, takes you to a small, closed-in room, strips you naked, and then sprays water on you. Or takes you into a bathroom, pulls your pants down, waits while you go, then tries to clean you up afterward. Things you've done by yourself, in private, for almost all your life. But you can't remember that you're unable to do these things independently anymore.

Learning to understand where the behavior is coming from and why for each resident, is an art form. Any nurse aide worth their salt gets to know their residents personally: their likes and dislikes in foods, clothing, and activities, their past life experiences that were special or meaningful to them, and their individual personality quirks. In any nursing home, it's the nurse aide who always knows the most about each resident's usual ability levels and Activities of Daily Living (ADLs). The aide is the greatest fountain of information on each resident anytime there's an emergency or special occasion. And they're the absolute best at caring for the residents they know. From getting them up and dressed in the morning to toileting and showering them, to whether they can feed themselves or need assistance with meals, to how they get from one place to another – can they walk, do they need a walker or cane, do they need to be transported via a wheelchair, can they stand, or do they need the help of a mechanical lift, etc. It's the nurse aide who knows all this and can do all this well with each resident in their charge.

I worked as a nurse aide on and off for about eight years before I got my nursing license. And I'm here to tell you it is some of the most rewarding work I've ever known. Working full-time causes the residents you're constantly taking care of to become almost as close as your own family. You celebrate holidays together, and you're there to help carry them through their heartaches.

That first nursing home was also where I learned about death. I cried with families as they said long goodbyes to their loved ones. I comforted one whose roommate of many years passed on. I sat with a resident, holding his hand through his final hours because he had no family and was afraid to die alone. After death occurred, a coworker and I cleansed the body of the deceased, dressed him in a patient gown, and placed his dentures, favorite ball cap, and favorite clothes in a bag at his feet. When the funeral home representative arrived, we helped him gently and reverently move the body to the funeral home transport cot, making sure his bag of clothes went too.

Looking back on it all these years later, I'm so glad I started out my nursing career as an aide. Not only did it teach me to give excellent personalized care, it also gave me the invaluable skill of learning to actually connect with each patient as a real person. To value the life and dignity of each one, no matter what their physical or mental limitations might be. It is my firm belief that all nurses should be required to work as nurse aides before completing their nursing training. It's not a very popular opinion to have. Too bad. In all my years in the medical field, it's been very obvious in almost every case whether the nurse had nurse aide training or not.

So yeah, my first job may have included 'wiping butts', but to those who are unable to see beyond that, I say this: I DARE you to go work as a nurse aide. You obviously have a lot to learn! Nurse aides, or CNAs as they're often called, are some of my biggest, brightest heroes!

CHAPTER TWO

When I was just barely 20, I had a sledding accident. I was at a weekend Christian youth camp, acting as a counselor for a section of a cabin of girls. It was wintertime in Michigan, which means lots of snow and snowbound fun. On Saturday morning, we rose up early and wore some warm clothes for a day of being mostly outside. It was a church camp, so we were on our way to the morning chapel service a few minutes before nine o'clock. I remember thinking to myself it would be a great morning to snuggle by a nice, warm fireplace with a cup of coffee. Instead, here I was, walking in the cold with a few giggling teenage girls.

Oh I loved those girls! They were mostly from my own home church, and I knew them well. I felt honored to get to be their counselor for the weekend. But I'm not a big fan of being really active first thing in the morning. I like to kind of ease gently into the day – with several cups of coffee. The girls, however, loved the sledding hill. Since it was right next to the chapel and we were a few minutes early, they started pleading with me to go down the hill with them.

"Just once," they begged. "Then we can all go inside where it's warm."

I caved. "Ok, just once. But then I'm headed for a cup of coffee."

They squealed with delight and grabbed a toboggan. We got on one at a time, sitting with our feet wrapped around and in the lap of the person in front of us, as sledding usually goes. I think there were four of us that ended up taking that ride.

That hill was fun! It was fairly steep, not too small, and ended in a smooth slide out over a frozen inland lake. I'd gone sledding down it many times before. I loved the feel of sliding so smoothly over the snow and then the snow-covered ice.

Unfortunately, this ride ended much differently. Near the bottom of the hill, we hit a bump and then a small drop-off. Horrible pain shot through me! I deliberately tipped sideways to bring the sled to a fast stop. I was crying out in pain, but it took several seconds for the girls to figure out that something was wrong. At first, they thought we'd simply capsized, and I was laughing. When they finally realized I was hurt, they started yelling for help. After a minute or so, I'd caught my breath enough to ask them to help me stand up.

Mistake. I took one step and screamed in pain, immediately going to my knees, then flat on my back in the snow. People rushed down the hill toward us. Someone got the message up the hill to call an ambulance. A few minutes later, I was strapped to a very uncomfortable backboard and being towed back up the hill on another toboggan. Hearing the huffing and puffing of the guys towing me, I was embarrassed. Though I wasn't really overweight, I sure did feel huge and fat then.

The camp was kind of out in the middle of nowhere. The ambulance crew was attentive, and the one driving took great care to make sure I suffered as few bumps as possible on the deeply pot-holed roads. They were very kind and a lot of fun, and they talked to me constantly to take my mind off the pain. I was taken to a small country hospital. There I suffered the humiliation of having the ED staff undress me and put a patient gown on me. I'd worn layers in readiness to be out in the cold, so it took some effort. In my mind were the hundreds of times I'd done that for all those residents I took care of in the nursing home I worked at. Now I knew what it felt like. I was completely unable to help them. Every move brought extreme pain to my back. Even taking a deep breath hurt me!

X-rays were no fun, either. They had to take pictures from a couple different angles, which meant more moving. When they got me settled back onto the ED cot, the doctor came in. I was frightened. By this age and with my limited nurse aide experience, I knew enough about back injuries to know how serious this could be. I faced him with dread that must have been obvious on my face.

"Well, young lady, you've had quite a morning!" He was a jovial man who had a great way of putting me at ease. "I've checked over your X-rays, and unfortunately, you have fractured one of the vertebrae in your back. I don't think it's too dangerous of a break, but we obviously want to be sure of that. You need further scans that we don't have the equipment for here."

"What does that mean?" I was confused. Was he saying I couldn't be treated? My anxiety stepped up a notch.

"I'm afraid I need to send you on another ambulance ride. We need to get you to a bigger hospital where they can complete the necessary tests, then you'll be brought back here."

My parents had arrived sometime during that ED stay, and I looked at them questioningly. They both nodded.

Mom knew I needed more than that. "We'll wait here, Honey. We'll be here when you get back." Reassured, I gave my attention back to the ED doctor.

"You'll have the same ambulance crew for your transport. They were worried about you and have been standing by in case you needed to take this trip. I'll order some pain medication to make it easier for you."

I was relieved. Those two guys were already special to me, and I trusted them.

So the phone call to the bigger hospital was made, the paperwork was signed, and I was medicated for the ride. I think the EMS crew told me the other hospital was about forty-five minutes away. I was pretty groggy for most of that trip. I vaguely remember joking with them and then seeing ceiling lights flying by overhead as they rolled my cot down the hallways of the hospital. I don't remember much else.

I think I spent two nights in the little country hospital. My time there was a blur of pain and worry. But my back fracture turned out to not be too severe, and I was fitted with a metal, slightly padded cage-of-a-brace for my torso. My dad turned the back end of our family station wagon into a bed, and I made the painful trip home lying down back there.

For a couple months, I had to wear the brace at all times whenever I was out of bed. That was my first experience of really needing assistance, having to learn to ask for and accept that help. Even simple things like brushing my teeth were suddenly hard to do. Have you ever realized how much you bend while brushing your teeth? It's really hard not to! And shaving my legs was impossible. I got in the bath, and Jetta did it for me.

I was forced to learn firsthand what it was really like to be a patient. It's not easy. It's constantly wanting and trying to do things yourself but not being able to. It's holding still and resting a lot, whether you feel like it or not. It's putting off asking for help as long as you can because you hate being a burden to your family.

Healing is a long, slow process. And no matter how much we wish it is otherwise, we – caregiver and care receiver alike – have to let it take all the time it needs to. I came out of that experience determined to give the best care I could to my patients.

CHAPTER THREE

Since then, my life has followed many varied paths. I graduated from college and got my nursing license in 1994 in Indiana. In the next few years, I worked in hospitals and nursing homes there, in Illinois, and finally, back home in Michigan. Nursing is never the same in two places. I mean, yeah, the same basic medical practices apply, but that's where it ends.

Nurses are notorious for 'eating their young' – treating newly graduated and beginner nurses pretty horribly. The cliques and backstabbing are usually more vicious than a TV season of Survivor. So it takes a good long while to feel comfortable. In my experience, the hospital environment is far worse about this. Maybe because there, everyone is always vying for the 'best' position. But in a nursing home, there is no 'best' position, and each employee desperately needs to know they can count on the others. Maybe for both those reasons plus a few.

But young as I was, I'd worked in the trenches as an aide. When the nastiness was aimed at me, I knew how to respond and how to protect myself. Also, there's a certain amount of steadfast credibility that comes with being a CNA. I knew what I knew and was secure in my abilities.

Anyway, I didn't wind up a casualty of the nursing notoriety machine like some of my classmates did. With a background in long-term caregiving, I was able to secure a job immediately upon graduation. It was in the hospital where I'd done most of my nursing clinicals. They had a unit set apart for long-term care patients needing a period of acute care. Tailor-made for my strengths, it was hard, demanding work, both mentally and physically, and I loved it.

As time passed, I worked at several nursing homes on different shifts. In Illinois, I worked at a Catholic hospital, again taking care of mostly long-term patients needing acute care. After moving to Michigan, I worked in more nursing homes. Eventually, I began working on a Medical/Surgical (Med/Surg.) unit in a tiny little country hospital. Problem was, they were short-staffed in the Emergency Department (ED). Being the nurse with the lowest seniority meant I was the one who got 'pulled' to help out there. Yikes! I'd never had any training in emergency medicine. I mean, I had to do a rotation of it in school, but the ED staff didn't trust green nursing students to do much, so we spent long hours kicking our heels just watching others work. Now I was expected to know a lot more than I was comfortable with. Talk about stress!

I learned fast. I had to. And it was great! I decided I really liked emergency care. After that, I worked at a couple more nursing homes and then became certified to teach CNA classes. For a few years, I got to pour into nurse aide students the wealth of experience I'd received thus far.

During that time, I became a CPR instructor and found in that a passion I didn't know I had. Over the next fourteen years or so, no matter what type of job I was working, I found time to teach hundreds of CPR/First Aid classes to different people from very different walks of life.

I was eventually hired as an adjunct professor to teach Medical Terminology classes for the local community college. Now there's a challenge. Medical jargons are often long and difficult, but I really enjoy words and language, and understanding them came easily to me. There were college students in those classes studying for different medical degrees. I tried hard to make the classes as fun and interesting as possible, because the bottom line is that no matter how you plan to use it in your career, spelling really counts.

There are several medical words that are spelled with only one letter difference, but their meanings are completely different. The words 'ileum' and 'ilium', for instance. The first one, containing the letter e, is the name for a section of the small intestine, while the second one, with two i's, is the name for the upper and largest of the three bones making up the hip and pelvic area. Unfortunately, many people find correct spelling to be extremely difficult. And then there are all the abbreviations. Medical abbreviations are a minefield for the unaware. So many of them can be used in more than one way, so context and great care are crucial in using them. We played a lot of word games, and I often tossed candy to the winners.

Volunteering as a licensed EMT on our local Emergency Medical Services (EMS) ambulance crew, I realized I had really missed emergency medicine. So I went back to working in an ED and kept up the EMS work. For several years I enjoyed doing both. I learned continually and honed a lot of skills I previously felt inadequate in. The constant unknown of what type of medical situation would occur next was stimulating. But after a time, it began to wear on me. I longed for a 'normal' life with a regular schedule.

Then came a stint of a few years as a Home Health/Hospice nurse, visiting patients in their homes to care for them. That job was great too! Taking care of someone in their environment, where their personal life really happens, is an entirely different world from hospital or nursing home care. Some for assistance with recovery and re-acclimation to home following recent surgery. Some for ongoing care of an IV or central line or for lab draws. Some for wound care and treatment. And some for end-of-life care, not only for the patient but for the family's preparation as well. That takes a very compassionate touch. And doing all of this with only the guidelines, experience, and limited supplies I could carry with me was challenging. I had to form a mindset completely different from that of working in an institution. One that makes me strong enough in my own skills and assets to be comfortable with knowing I couldn't just step out into the hall and almost immediately have a whole medical team there with me. I had to learn how to problem-solve on a whole new level. It was really daunting at first, but I came to enjoy the autonomy of it and took pride in my successes.

Finally, the surgical department...

I'd been interested in working in surgery for several years but didn't have the guts to try it. I wish now that I'd done it a whole lot sooner. And now, after twenty-seven years of working as a registered nurse in all kinds of healthcare settings and all hours of the day and night, I finally landed my dream job. Circulating in various operating rooms during surgeries fascinated me. General surgeries, orthopedic surgeries, spinal surgeries, C-sections, even endoscopies and colonoscopies; I enjoyed them all. But my favorite was the recovery room. There was just something special about getting to monitor and take care of the needs of patients as they slowly awoke from anesthesia.

Always a quick learner, I had no problem understanding computerized charting. That was the easy part. Meeting and assessing patients, reviewing paperwork, and transferring patients from one bed to another... these were also expected and familiar tasks.

The rest, however, was all new. I had to learn to set up each surgical room with the necessary machinery and sterile equipment. One of the biggest challenges to this process was actually locating the specific items a surgeon required for each type of surgery. The supply room was huge! It took a long time to feel confident there. It also took a lot of trial and error to become familiar with the process of unwrapping and presenting sterile equipment in the correct ways. Then there was the process of preparing each patient for surgery. The circulating nurse was responsible for positioning the patient correctly for their specific operation and completing the necessary cleansing of the surgical site – often under the watchful eye of the surgeon. And as a surgical room gets used several times in a row for different kinds of operations, I had to master the art of the quick turnaround of the room between procedures.

There were so many new skills to hone; so much new information to process. I'd spent the past several months being trained in this role, and I absolutely loved it! The world of the surgery department was very different from anything in my experience. I was learning, learning, learning, and happily soaking it all up.

CHAPTER FOUR

But something was VERY wrong and growing worse almost daily. It scared me that I couldn't control or figure out how to stop it. I couldn't breathe! No matter how often I paused for a few seconds to catch my breath, it was never enough. I couldn't go on like this. I had to find a way to breathe! And tired? I'd apparently never known the meaning of the word! I was exhausted – always.

Meanwhile, I strove for 'business as usual'. Having been a very conscientious nurse, I tried to give my best in whatever job I had, helping out my coworkers as much as my own duties allowed. I usually made it my mission to bring a smile to their faces through personal compliments and noticing their needs. Now I had nothing to give. I struggled to make it through minute by minute. And though still forcing myself to remain cheerful, I had literally no reserves. Nothing extra. Not even enough for myself.

Reluctantly, my heart pounding, I finally went to my manager's office at the end of a long work day. Sinking into the chair facing the desk, I tried unsuccessfully to calm my nerves. I had to force myself to make eye contact.

"I'm sorry. I can't do this anymore."

My manager was shocked. "What? Why?! You're doing so well!"

"Thank you. I know I just had my review and told you I love this job and planned to keep doing this for many years. I do love it! This is the job I've always wanted."

"Then what's wrong? Did something happen?"

"Yes and no." I struggled to find the words to explain. "I think I'm having panic attacks. I get here and start working, and within ten minutes, I'm short of breath and extremely anxious. I'm jittery with anxiety but completely exhausted all the time I'm here."

"Is it the staff? All the nurses love working with you. And none of the surgeons have complained. In fact, several of them have complimented you. They like having you in the room."

I shook my head, inwardly reveling in the positive affirmations while also battling the unfairness of this. "No, everyone has been really nice! They've all been so patient with me and all my questions." It was true. Every nurse, every surgical tech, every anesthesiologist, and most of the surgeons had been not only nice to me but patiently instructive.

I leaned forward with my forearms on my knees, trying to discreetly ease my breathing. "I don't know what's wrong. I've worked for the ambulance service and in the emergency department, both for several years. Stressful situations are the norm in those places. I never get anxious at work! But now I can't breathe, and I can't get the anxiety under control. I don't know what else to do. I think I'm going to have to find a different job."

The manager and I both sat silent for a few moments. Neither wanted the conversation to end this way.

"Look, how about you and I both give it a little thought, and maybe we can come up with a workable solution. You're a really good nurse. I'd really hate to lose you." My manager looked at me hopefully, and I nodded in response. What else could I do?

"Ok. I don't want to leave, but I don't know what other option there is."

It took several days. For me, those days were a struggle. Physically I felt my body was fighting a losing battle for every breath and movement, while emotionally, I was grieving the possibility of having to leave this dream job and all the coworkers I'd come to like and respect.

Then one day, my manager called me into her office. I entered to find Leah – the surgery department's second-in-command and one of my favorite nurses – already seated and waiting.

"I think we may have come up with an idea," my manager began. "Leah tells me you really enjoy working in the recovery room. She says your experience and care for patients really shine when you're in there."

Leah chimed in. "That's a much less physically demanding role. You would be holding still and monitoring patients most of the time, and you'd only have to walk a few steps to get them medications if they need something."

"So how about we assign you to the recovery room full-time? Do you think that would work for you?"

Relief and excitement flooded my heart. "Yes! I'd love that! But would that work with the other nurses?"

Leah laughed. "Most of them hate working in the recovery room and only do it when they have to. I think you'll become the instant hero as soon as they get the news."

"So you'll do it then?" My manager was all smiles. "That'll work for you? We get to keep you here?"

I didn't even try to contain my own smile. "Absolutely!"

Three months went by. My breathing didn't get any easier, and my anxiety was still constantly out of control. But at least I was still getting to do the job I loved. After the exhaustion of transferring a patient from a surgical room, I got to at least partially recoup for a while during their recovery period. I'd found my niche. I actually looked forward to work these days. I felt confident and professional during the day and went home feeling accomplished. I just knew this was the job I wanted to keep for the rest of my nursing career.

But it was not to be...

CHAPTER FIVE

As all medically minded people tend to do, I tried over and over to figure out by myself what was wrong. But nothing seemed to fit my symptoms. I couldn't decide exactly what the problem was. Finally, I made an appointment with my primary care provider for my delayed yearly checkup. My 'doctor', Kelly, was a friend who'd worked side by side with me in the Emergency Department trenches while also working toward her Nurse Practitioner license. Becoming her regular patient when she entered practice had been a no-brainer since trust had already been established. She was easy to share confidence with and very thorough. Having such a close provider was a rare privilege. So now, when my need was so urgent, there was no dread of a yearly checkup.

Having turned 50 last December, I had put off getting my routine physical due to the upheaval caused by the international outbreak of the COVID-19 virus. I finally had the physical in late June. It all went smoothly, with nothing unusual found, so I was surprised to receive a call from Kelly the following day.

"Jessie, we just got your labs back, and your hemoglobin level has dropped dramatically from 13 down to 8. That's a dangerous level. We need to find out what's causing it. I'm afraid we need to schedule you for a colonoscopy as soon as possible."

Hmmm... Ugh... Ok...

By now, I'd assisted with many colonoscopies and knew what having one entailed. But this was different! This was me. It would be humiliating enough if the surgical team were complete strangers. But these were my coworkers. People I worked side by side with every day.

My belly felt fine. Well, my version of fine. Sure, I had frequent bouts of loose stools, and my stools were unpredictable, but that'd been happening for several years – ever since I'd had my gallbladder removed. I'd had no pain and had never noticed any bleeding with it. *Can't I just skip this and pretend I didn't know I needed it?* But Kelly, thorough as ever, had already ordered the procedure. There was no getting out of it. This was a no-win situation.

Hiding in the bathroom before starting work, I tried to give myself a pep talk. *Ok, girl. You've got it to do. Just get it over with! All you have to do is walk out there and tell the scheduler you have an order to schedule a colonoscopy. No big deal. You can do this! Now go!!*

I forced my feet to obey. Step by step, I slowly approached the scheduler. Somehow I forced the words out.

"I need to schedule a colonoscopy." There! First hurdle done.

Erica was in charge of making up the plan of surgeries for each upcoming week. In the middle of making last-minute adjustments to today's schedule, she merely glanced up at me. "Ok, when do you want to schedule it for?"

I felt myself flush. *Never!* "My doctor already put the order in and said I need it as soon as possible."

Erica pulled out the schedule. "We're pretty full right now. Unless it's an emergency, the earliest I can get you in is Thursday, August 6th. Is that ok?"

"Um, sure. What do I need to do to get those two days off?"

Erica waved a hand. "Oh, no problem. We'll just pull another nurse to work in the recovery room those two days. What time of day do you wanna do it?"

"As early as possible." *So there'll be lots of patients after me, and they won't remember mine.*

"That's what I'd do too. Ok, you'll be the first patient of the day next Thursday, August 6th. The pre-op nurse will get with you a few days before and make sure all your information is correct. She'll also give you the pre-op instructions then and confirm your time."

I somehow managed to mumble a quiet "Thank you." Erica waved her hand again and went back to working on today's schedule. No big deal – to her.

But just like that, the first step was over with. Now the true dread began. My name would appear on the surgery schedule. Everyone would know I was having a colonoscopy.

I was generally a quiet person and very private. But I enjoyed my job immensely. I honestly liked and respected my coworkers, something not always a given in healthcare. But I was happiest being behind the scenes. I gave my best at work and chatted easily and readily with my colleagues, but I always preferred to stay out of the spotlight. I was friendly but still a bit shy and introverted.

At fifty years old and carrying a little extra weight, not to mention all the sagging, scars, and stretch marks, I had no desire to remove my clothes, don a patient gown, and go through with this very personally-invasive procedure with my coworkers present. On the other hand, I had such great respect for the general surgeons on staff, the surgical team members, and the outpatient staff that I wouldn't want anyone else to do the procedure. Again, a no-win situation.

Kelly had also ordered a mammogram. It was time to update my checkup. *YUCK!! I hate those. So uncomfortable and personal.* However, I went through with the mammogram in late July. Everything was clear. I breathed a sigh of relief. Of all that could be going wrong with my body right now, I knew I wasn't ready for problems from the mammogram.

And then my younger brother had a heart attack. His wife, Gemma, called our parents to give the family the news. Sunday afternoon, just four days before my colonoscopy was scheduled, Les was rushed to the hospital and into the cardiac catheterization lab. They found two life-threatening blockages and put in stents. My family was in shock. Nothing big like that had ever happened in our family. *How could this happen?! He just got the Regional Director job. That role is perfect for him with his gifts. Oh, God, thank You for sparing his life! We could have lost him so quickly!*

The next day the work week began. My dread seemed to grow by the hour. Anxiety was too tame a word for what I felt now. I had to keep telling myself this was no big deal. Lots of colonoscopies were done every week. Mine would be impersonal and unremarkable, just one of many. Funny how the brain works. I was dreading the humiliation of the procedure itself – but never really allowed myself to even remotely consider the different possible findings it could produce.

On Wednesday, I did the prep as ordered, knowing I'd have to follow it to the letter in order for my colon to be as clean as possible. It was awful. Taking the stool softeners and drinking the prescribed mixtures was the easy part. After that came hour upon hour of cramps and diarrhea.

It was almost a relief to check in to be the day's first patient before dawn Thursday morning. My mom was officially listed as the designated driver and accompanied me to the hospital. She waited in the pre-op room throughout the procedure and was there to assist when I returned after the colonoscopy.

The time seemed to go in slow motion as we checked in and were shown to our assigned outpatient room. One of my favorite coworkers, a friendly nurse named Chloe, came in to complete the paperwork, get me changed into a patient gown, and settle on a surgical cot. She then started the IV and drew labs. Next came the required visits from the nurse, the anesthesiologist, and the surgeon to make sure my mom and I had all the necessary information about the procedure and to make sure I was ready. Finally, it was time. My mom said a prayer over me that I didn't hear, then she hugged me just before I was wheeled out of the room, already becoming sleepy from the anesthesia medication. All just exactly as expected.

I awoke in the outpatient room with my mom beside me. I was dimly aware of the sober, even saddened, faces of the surgical team – my coworkers – as one of them said something kind, and they left the room. That seemed alarming and effectively woke me up. I was sitting up waiting when the surgeon came into the room. His face was grave.

"There's a tumor… nearly blocking the colon… almost positive it's cancerous… surgery to remove it as soon as possible… almost certain chemotherapy will be needed…"

Though still a little groggy from the anesthesia and feeling the first edges of alarm from those words, the only response coming from the depths of my soul was faith. God, please just get glory from this! That was all I could say. Immediately I felt a deep, calming peace. Still facing the surgeon, I heard the rest of his report. Biopsies had been taken, and results would come in a few days. *So much for my coworkers not remembering my colonoscopy. They'll never forget this.*

The ride home was a blur, as were the various phone calls my parents were making to our close-knit family to inform them.

That was Thursday. A day like no other. A date I'd always remember.

CHAPTER SIX

I had thankfully taken Friday off and was not scheduled for weekends, so I spent the next two days trying to process it all. But I knew I wasn't making much progress. *This is crazy! This was supposed to be just a routine checkup! What are you doing, God?!* I was fifty years old, had been divorced for twelve years, and had two adult children. And now, suddenly, I was facing the possibility of never seeing 51. Deep in the fog of shock and fear, I had no idea how to tell my son and daughter.

They were almost complete opposites. Jude, 24, had graduated college two years before and then spent a two-year stint in Japan, where he'd worked at a school teaching English as a second language. He was now back in the States and getting ready to go to grad school. While Jude was very liberal in his thinking, Jamie was very conservative.

Jamie was now 21 and worked for a missions organization on the West Coast. She had already co-led teams on missions trips and had been to several foreign countries to share Jesus' love. Both were bona fide world travelers, and both were strong-willed and independent. But though their viewpoints were at opposite poles, they had each made it a priority to stay in contact with both their parents. I loved talking on the phone with whichever one happened to call. I was so proud of them.

But a mom is a mom! It doesn't matter how old your kids get or how far they move away. A mom protects her kids! I struggled and fought with myself. *I can't just pick up the phone and say, "Hey, how's it going? That's nice. Oh, by the way, I have a tumor. It might be cancer..." But I can't NOT tell them!* Finally, I all but chickened out. I typed out a message and sent it to both of them at once, and of course, they both reacted with shock and fear and questions I couldn't answer yet.

I felt horrible about it. But what else could I do? Every time I tried to talk to someone about it, I seemed to somehow run out of words and close up inside. Interactions with others seemed unreal. Like the rest of the world was still going on as usual, but I myself had stopped. Inside, I was curling up in a ball and trying to shut the scary world out.

But true avoidance wasn't an option.

On Sunday, I went to church, as usual, trying for outward normalcy during an inward hurricane. It wasn't easy. My family was now on the prayer chain, and several people wanted to talk and pray with me. Finally, I was able to escape to the family lunch gathering.

In past years, Sunday family lunches had often been huge, including me and my parents, my brother Les with his wife Gemma and their son Ian, my sister Jetta with her husband Bill and their two adult children, Sarah and Heath, any other family that happened to be around, plus any friends someone had invited. Often, there were over a dozen people present. But since COVID, the gathering had become small, and now, it usually only consisted of me, my parents, Bill and Jetta. Today, our little lunch gathering was quiet and emotional. As the five of us sat around the table, we shared some of our personal thoughts and feelings.

I didn't say much. In fact, I tried hard to say as little as possible. The turmoil inside me was too huge, too deep, too unknown. I didn't know how to get a handle on it, how to wrap my brain around it. And Les had had a heart attack! It was easier to focus on that than to even acknowledge the chaos in my mind. As horrible as that sounds, I couldn't help it.

Last Sunday, we'd gotten the call that my younger brother Les had just had a heart attack. Still reeling from that shock, there was now the possibility of me having cancer. After a lifetime of almost no major problems, our family was now facing two huge medical life threats in one week. It felt heavy and foreign. We were so very close, always instinctively leaning in toward each other and, most of all, on God. It was a time for the family to join hands around the table in deep, heartfelt prayer. All at once, life seemed so very precious and extremely precarious.

I spent that Sunday afternoon with Shelly. Her son, Matt, had gone to high school with my kids, and he was now one of my best friends. He'd gone through a very rough couple of years, and despite the age difference, we'd somehow forged a strong bond of trusting friendship during that time. Along the way, I met his family and became close friends with his mom and sister. Coming to know and love them over the past few years, I now spend as much time as possible with them.

The two of us rode around in Shelly's pickup truck, running errands and talking about life. She was very down-to-earth but had the unique ability to not let the troubles of that earth keep her down. As only a good friend can, Shelly had me laughing and feeling lighter than I had in days. We returned to my house around dinner time, joking with each other about our adult kids as we carried a few odds and ends into the house.

And then, suddenly, without warning, my breathing changed. Though always short of breath these days, something had radically worsened. Now I really couldn't get enough air in!

"Jessie!! What's wrong?!" Shelly grabbed a chair and lowered me into it. Through the panic, I panted, "Can't breathe! Go get Abbie and have her take my blood pressure!"

Shelly ran. Out the door, across the wide driveway, and up the little hill to the neighbor's house.

Aaron and Abbie were wonderful neighbors to me. Time and again, they'd surprised me with the help I needed but was too introverted to ask for. Aaron faithfully kept my big driveway plowed in winter and several times mowed my huge lawn when my riding machine had broken down. Abbie ran a daycare in their home. She often gave me baked goods and ingredients for various meals. Both Aaron and Abbie stopped to talk with me several times a week when they saw me outside. They made me welcome in their home, their pool, and their family get-togethers. Both were EMTs and volunteered for the local rural Fire and Rescue department.

Now Shelly didn't hesitate. She ran up the steps and right into the house. Abbie looked up and saw the panicked look on her face, but before she could even ask what was wrong, Shelly rapidly spat out the words. "Come quick! Something's wrong with Jessie! She can't breathe! Oh, wait! Bring your blood pressure cuff!"

Abbie wasted no time. She scrambled to find the BP cuff, a stethoscope, and shoes. Shelly had already run back toward my house and was yelling, "Hurry!"

Still not breathing well, I was pale and felt cold and panicky. My breathing was fast and shallow as I struggled to pull in enough air. Abbie, fumbling a little with the BP cuff because she was scared for me, soon announced my blood pressure was 156/96. Quite high compared to my normal range.

Shelly wasn't taking 'no' for an answer. "Let's go!" She and Abbie grabbed my purse and walked me to Shelly's truck. While she drove the twenty-five minutes to the hospital, I called my mom.

"Hello?"

"Hi, Mom, it's me."

"Jessie, are you ok? You don't sound good."

"I'm having some trouble breathing. Shelly's taking me to the Emergency Department. Can you meet me there?"

"Oh no! Of course! Dad and I will be on our way shortly. I love you, Jessie! We'll be praying."

"Thanks, Mom. I love you too."

Arriving at the hospital ED entrance, Shelly helped me inside and then went to park the truck. I had worked in this ED for a few years and knew almost all the staff well. Still having difficulty breathing, I was immediately escorted back to a private room so the nurse could begin assessing me. Shelly sat at my bedside and explained to the nurse what had happened, stressing how suddenly my breathing problem had begun. The nurse quickly measured my vital signs, started an IV, and drew some blood. She also got me changed into a patient gown and put a nasal cannula on me to provide me oxygen. Sometime in the flurry of activity, my parents arrived, and Shelly left the room so my mom could be there.

CHAPTER SEVEN

As the doctor entered and began a thorough assessment, my mom explained about the colonoscopy and what had been found. Tests were ordered, and I was instructed to focus on calming my breathing down. The doctor and nurse left the room, turning the lights down a little to help me relax. I closed my eyes. Though my mom was silent now, I knew she was praying. I decided to concentrate on Jesus, too, instead of on breathing. Peace washed over me even though it was still hard work to breathe. *Father, thank You for being here in this hospital room with me! I can feel Your amazing Presence and peace. Please help me! Please comfort Mom! And whatever happens, what matters most to me is that You get glory from all this.*

After a while, a nurse came in to see if we needed anything. I shook my head, and my mom agreed. The nurse made sure my call light was within reach, then left the room to check in some new arrivals. A few minutes later, my breathing suddenly got even worse.

"Mom, go get help!"

My mom hurried to the door but couldn't see anyone at the desk or in the hallway. "There's no one to ask, Jessie."

"NOW, Mom, I need help NOW!!"

"HELP!" I heard my usually quiet-voiced mom yelling in the hallway out by the desk. "Somebody HELP!! My daughter can't breathe!"

Two nurses and the doctor came running. I was in full panic, fighting for air. The room was starting to go dark at the edges of my vision. I felt like I was under water, drowning, and couldn't get to the people trying to save me. Everything was fuzzy and dim. I felt people moving around me, putting an oxygen mask on me, and doing other things. Everyone was talking at once, but the sound seemed distant and jumbled. I had no idea what was happening. The darkening room was spinning away from me, and I had no point of reference to hold onto.

And then suddenly, I did. One quiet voice was talking calmly in my ear.

"Jessie, you have to breathe." It was the voice of Mandy, one of the ED nurses I knew well. "Don't fight it. Just take a breath. That's good. Now another one. Good. Now slow it down a little at a time. That's right. You're going to be ok. Slow it down some more. Good…"

Slowly the room came back into focus as my vision cleared, and I looked around.

"What happened?"

"That's what we're going to find out." The doctor finished listening to my lungs and, with a serious look on his face, said, "I think a CT scan of the chest is in order, given that little scare. I'll go put the order in."

"How do you feel?" Mom was once more beside me, holding my hand. She had tears in her eyes. I immediately shied away from the thought of what it must be like to watch helplessly as your child went through something like that, especially with no medical training. It must have been horrifying for her! I couldn't stop the tears from spilling over my own eyes.

Through the shortness of breath, I managed a few words. "I don't know. That was so scary! My body feels like lead, like I've been doing hard physical labor for hours. But I'm also all jittery. And pretty nauseated."

One of the nurses was still in the room. "I'll ask the doctor to order some anti-nausea medication and something to relax you. I'll be right back."

Alone with Mom again, I began to tremble.

"Mom, that was terrifying! I don't EVER wanna feel like that again!"

"Oh, Baby," Mom wept, "I hope it never happens again! That was horrible!"

She leaned over the hospital bed rail and wrapped her arms around me. Burying my tear-streaked face in Mom's shoulder, I clung to that hug until most of the trembling passed. "I'm so glad you're here, Mom. I love you."

"I love you too. And I wouldn't be anywhere else at a time like this. I'm glad I can be here for you."

A few minutes later, I was taken, bed and all, to have the CT scan of my chest. It didn't take long, but I saw and understood the huge relief on Mom's face as I returned to our room in the ED.

And then the wait... I prayed and tried to relax and concentrate on breathing.

Eventually, the doctor returned, entering and closing the door. "Well, the CT scan shows you have a blood clot in each lung. We'll be starting a heparin drip, and you'll have to be admitted to the hospital for two or three days."

My nurse-brain kicked into overdrive. *Blood clots in the lungs?! Pulmonary emboli?! That's life-threatening!! I could have died right here in this bed a few minutes ago!! No way can I let Mom know THAT!!*

Through long years of medical practice, I managed to keep my face smooth and serious.

"Wow. Scary. Ok."

The doctor lingered. "Given your recent history and what we've just learned, would you like me to see if the biopsy results from your colonoscopy are back yet?"

Keep it together, Jessie! Your mom's here.

"Yes, please."

"Ok, I'll go put in your admission orders and see if I can find the biopsy results. I'll be back in a few minutes." The doctor stepped out of the room.

I had nowhere to hide as Mom searched my face.

"How serious is that, Jessie?"

God, please give me words!

"It's very serious, Mom. Depending on the size and location of the clot, it can be fatal. But they've caught it and the heparin drip is the right thing to do."

Mom sat back in her chair and was quiet for a few moments. And then came the gentle, expected, "How are you doing with all of this, Jessie?"

My eyes closed, still focused on trying to breathe calmly, I shrugged.

"What can I say, Mom? It's pretty overwhelming. Physically, I feel pretty icky. Emotionally, I'm kind of numb. Mentally, I'm going all over the place – remembering patients I took care of with similar problems, analyzing each order and decision the doctor and nurses make, wondering how to tell my kids, wondering about finances, etc… I don't know. This isn't like anything I've ever tried to handle before. But I do know one thing. God is still on the throne. He's still in control. He's right here in this room. If only one good thing comes out of all this, I want it to be that He gets glory from it."

"Amen." Mom's voice was tearful, but quiet. Peaceful after the storm.

As soon as the doctor opened the door and I saw his face, I knew. It was bad news.

He took a seat in the chair at my bedside opposite my mom. I found my complete attention was held by the sheets of paper in his hand.

Once again, he asked, "Do you still want the results?"

My eyes met Mom's, and we both nodded. I braced myself as I turned to face the doctor, already sure what he was going to say.

He didn't mince words. "The tumor is indeed malignant. I'm sorry. The pulmonary clots made me suspect this. Cancer sometimes causes blood clots."

I nodded and dropped my eyes. *Breathe, Jessie… It's not like you didn't expect it after what the surgeon said.* But hearing it confirmed, out loud, made it so much more definite. So much scarier. I felt my mom squeeze my hand while I searched for the strength to hear the rest. The doctor waited patiently, quietly, until I was able to meet his eyes again. Knowing I was a nurse, he handed me the biopsy results printout and pointed to the line containing the diagnosis.

"Invasive adenocarcinoma."

There it was, spelled out in black and white. *Colon cancer.*

Amazingly, I suddenly felt indescribable peace surrounding me, almost like a cocoon. Though my breathing was only slightly easier, I felt as if I'd fallen into a cottony cloud that, instead of suffocating me, surrounded and supported me. And once again, my heart responded in faith and love. *"God, please just get glory from this."*

After a little more discussion, the doctor again stepped out of the room, and my mom once again wrapped her arms around my shoulders. "I'm so proud of you, Honey! We're going to get through this. All of us together. You're not facing this alone."

Prayers, praises, and tears mingled together as two hearts poured out our love to such an amazing Almighty God who could bring indescribable peace of faith in the presence of nearly overwhelming fear.

CHAPTER EIGHT

Early the next morning, I awoke in my hospital room. It felt strange to be alone after all that had happened. I knew it wouldn't last. Soon hospital staff would come in to once again take my vital signs for the umpteenth time, assess my lungs, give me medications, adjust my IV… Soon my mom or sister would arrive to sit at my bedside and talk with me, pray with me, play games with me, comfort me… But in the quietness of this moment, instead of enjoying my brief solitude as I always did, I began to feel the heaviness of the two new diagnoses.

Bilateral Pulmonary Emboli.

Colon Cancer.

That was the first time I began to realize the new truth: life would never be the same. If I survived, the aftermath would be extensive. Oncology appointments, specialists, medications, therapies. I wondered how many people already knew. Had my parents called my kids? Had they updated the prayer chain at church? Did my surgery coworkers know yet?

Quietly, I laid my head back and closed my eyes. *Father, please carry me. I can't do this alone.* The beloved words of one of my favorite Rich Mullins songs ran through my head as a heartfelt prayer. *"Hold me, Jesus, cuz I'm shaking like a leaf. You have been King of my glory. Would You be my Prince of Peace?"*

Soon the door opened, and a nurse walked in pushing a cart with a computer and some medications on it. She introduced herself and then proceeded to do a full assessment, including vital signs. She was efficient and friendly, making fun of herself when her fingers fumbled at the keyboard, and I soon found myself smiling.

"I see you're still a bit short of breath, Jessie. Did anything they gave you last night help you breathe easier?"

"The Valium helped some. The Zofran sure does help with the nausea too."

"Great. I brought the Zofran. Let me see..." She checked the computer. "Yes, you do have an order for Valium. I'll go get that as soon as I give you the Zofran and check your heparin drip."

By the time she'd given me the dose of Valium, breakfast had arrived. I had almost no appetite, but I knew I had to get something into my system with the meds. I certainly didn't want to make everything worse by vomiting. I settled for coffee and pudding as I was on a soft diet to ease digestion due to the size and location of the tumor.

Jetta walked in and caught me grimacing at the taste of the hospital's instant coffee.

"What? No Starbucks? The least you could've done was bring me some decent coffee!"

Jetta laughed. "Nope. I just had to see the look on your face when you tasted that stuff. How's my baby sister this morning?"

"Ugh. I don't know. Do I really have to answer that with this horrible taste still in my mouth?" I pulled another face at my sister, and we both laughed. My addiction to coffee was lifelong, stemming from my earliest childhood when I used to climb up on my daddy's lap every morning at breakfast and 'help' him drink his coffee. There was just something yummy and comforting about the smell of good coffee. I could most often be found with my hands cradling a warm mug of my favorite brew. My family and friends teased me about it, but they also kept me pretty well supplied with both coffee and coffee mugs.

"So, what's on the agenda for today?" Jetta asked.

"I'm not sure. I don't think much of anything except lab draws every few hours. The doctor hasn't been in yet."

"Cool, then we can have some good talks and play some games. I brought some Scrabble tiles and a few other things. Oh, I brought your cell phone charger and your Bible too."

I actually cheered. "Yay! You're the absolute best!"

With that, the two of us settled down to play the family's favorite form of Scrabble. We mixed up the tiles in the middle of the over-the-bed table, flipped them all face down, then each drew ten tiles. One of us said, "Ready?" and the other said, "Go!" Then we flipped over our own ten tiles and began to build intersecting words with them as fast as we could. As soon as one of us used up all her tiles, they'd call out, "Draw!" and each of us drew two more tiles. We did this until all the tiles were used up. The first one to successfully intersect words using all their tiles won. Per family tradition, we compared our structures of intersecting words at the end of the game, exclaiming and playfully arguing over which one of us had come up with the most creative words.

We played five or six games before I got too tired. *Wow, I have no stamina! No wonder I was always so short of breath at work and needed to rest so often. I wonder how long those clots have been there and how big they are.*

Jetta saw both the apology and the fear in my eyes. "Ok, rest time. You lay back and close your eyes, and I'll sit here and read my book."

"Actually, Jetta, would you mind reading the Bible to me awhile? Maybe a couple of Psalms. I want to read because I know it would relax me, but I'm so tired."

"Of course, I'll read our favorite book to you! Any specific Psalms you'd like to hear?" Jetta opened my Bible and turned to the book of Psalms.

I smiled. "Surprise me."

Jetta smiled, too, and turned to Psalm 103 and began to read. "Praise the LORD, O my soul; all my inmost being, praise his holy name..." She read the Psalm through and then turned to Psalm 139 and began again. "O LORD, you have searched me, and you know me..." And as Jetta's sweet, quiet voice settled God's Word over me like a soothing blanket, I drifted into a gentle sleep.

Two days later, after another set of CT scans, I was finally released from the hospital. I'd received several prescriptions for new medications and had been taught to give myself painful blood thinner injections in my abdomen twice a day. Any activity still caused me shortness of breath, so by the time we arrived at my parents' house, I needed a nap. Too tired to climb the stairs, I laid down on the couch and was soon deeply asleep.

I woke to the sounds of Jetta and my parents talking quietly at the dining room table. Reluctantly I got up and joined them. Wrapping my trembling hands around the warm mug of coffee my dad brought me, I braced myself. I knew what was coming.

"Honey, we're wondering if maybe you should move in here for a while." My mom said the words as gently as possible. She phrased it as a suggestion, but I knew they'd all come to this same conclusion.

Jetta reached over and took my hand in hers. "You're so weak already, Baby, and taking care of your house and yard..."

"And chemotherapy treatments certainly aren't going to make it any easier. I hate to bring that up, but we're pretty sure at this point that's what we're headed for, right?" My dad had a knack for bringing out the major issues and saying what needed to be said in such a straightforward way, but it was, nevertheless, laced with the greatest kindness and spoken with extreme gentleness. He had tears in his eyes, and his voice was gravelly from trying to contain his emotions.

I took a deep, fortifying breath. "I've given this a lot of thought over the past few days. I know this is going to need to happen." My voice broke. Swallowing hard, I worked to get the rest out, "I'm just not ready yet. I need a little time to process. It's all happening so fast. I need some alone time." Looking at Jetta, I said, "And I need lake time."

They all understood. The shores of Lake Michigan were only fifteen minutes away, and we two girls often escaped to our favorite beach there. A lot of soul-searching, prayer, and long talks happened in that beautiful place.

"We'll go as soon as possible," Jetta promised. "You need to rest today. Maybe we can go tomorrow after your appointment with the surgeon. We'll see. I'll make sure the beach chairs are in my van so we can go whenever it works out."

Looking at my parents, I once again had to work hard to speak. "I also made a decision. If the surgeon says I need chemotherapy, I'll plan to move in with you before chemo treatments start."

I heard Mom's sigh of relief. "I really think that's the right decision, Honey. You're going to need our help."

I just nodded, unable to speak. Jetta leaned closer, wrapped her arms around me, and just held me awhile. She, more than anyone, knew what my solitude meant to me.

CHAPTER NINE

So that's it, then? That's what I'm headed for? Is it ever going away? Will I ever get my life back? And what happens after? What about my kids? Will I ever see my grandkids? What if I lose my job or can't work anymore? What if I'm sick for the rest of my life? I don't wanna always be a burden to my wonderful family! I don't wanna be useless! What if it goes away and then comes back? Am I ready to die? What if…? What if…? What if…?

Feeling stunned and overwhelmed with questions, I sat staring out over the lush green grass and tall pines in the backyard of my three-bedroom home. This was my oasis. I loved this place: the quiet solitude; the soft breezes whispering through the trees; the afternoon sun slanting through the surrounding forest to splash warm strips of gold on the yard, deepening the multitude of colors until I could almost feel each one. This was my retreat from the world, my safe place. The one place I could completely let my guard down and allow my emotions to flow freely. And now… what? Would I wind up losing this place? Would I be forced to sell the house I'd spent so much time and effort – not to mention all my meager savings – setting up and decorating just the way I had always wanted?

As the questions grew, so did the fear.

I had no answers.

Cancer... Blood clots in my lungs...

Just four days after my little brother had a heart attack...

Sitting there on the swing on my backyard deck, I couldn't help but feel like my mind was on a merry-go-round. *Colon cancer... blood clots... surgery... chemo... colon cancer... blood clots... surgery... chemo...* I struggled not to think about the possible implications of each, but I'd been a nurse too long. I knew too much. I understood a lot of the medical *what if's*. That was when I began to face the fact that the 'normal' I'd always taken for granted wasn't coming back for a long time, if ever. Depression set in like a heavy weight. I finally gave in to tears, full of fear and the beginnings of grief.

I thought a strained marriage was really hard. Struggling through the lonely aftermath of divorce and broken dreams – most of which, I now admit, I caused through my own immature selfishness. Lost and hurting, I made a lot of bad decisions during that time. I'd still been recovering from the messes I made and wishing I'd handled a lot of things better – when the Empty Nest freight train hit me full force. My kids graduated high school and moved out into the big wide world. And with them went the main focus and purpose of my whole adult life. I thought I wouldn't survive the emptiness and loneliness during that time. That first year truly alone had been the hardest of my life.

But CANCER?!?! How in the world am I going to get through this?! I have a house to take care of and bills to pay! How am I going to do this alone? What if I have to be off work for a long time? And what will happen to me physically? What's it like to lose all your hair? Will I be in pain? I felt like a swarm of angry bees was attacking my mind and stinging me with all kinds of anxiety.

And then suddenly, the still, small voice I'd come to know and love whispered, *"In this world you will have trouble. But take heart! I have overcome the world"* (John 16:33). One of my all-time favorite verses. I was suddenly very thankful for the many Scriptures I'd taken the time to memorize in my childhood and teen years. Though the depression didn't disappear, I now discovered a deep peace was permeating my soul.

God was not surprised by this cancer. He wasn't wringing His hands, anxiously wondering how He was going to handle it. He had already overcome it! Before it ever even started! And I had never been meant to handle it alone. Though I often struggled with overwhelming loneliness and feeling unlovable because of my divorce and bad decisions, still I really was not alone! In His strength, and with my family surrounding me, I would get through this. One step at a time.

With that voice and amazing peace came the realization of the breakthrough that happened without me even realizing it. Having grown up in the Christian home of a devoted pastor and in the arms of a family full of love and acceptance, I had nevertheless become a rebellious and selfish person. I then allowed that person to wreak havoc in my heart, my home, and every aspect of my life. Both I and everyone around me suffered. And the depth of those wounds continually haunted me.

But I finally came to my senses and grew up. Though I'd wandered far and done a lot of horrible things, I still always carried deep within me the knowledge that there is most definitely a very real and absolute God. And somehow, through all my ugliness, He still loved me. Completely. Unconditionally.

I suddenly remembered the birth of my first child, the wonder I'd felt when they placed my perfect little newborn son in my arms. At that moment, I'd experienced a sudden fierce protectiveness that knew no bounds. As I stared at his beautiful little scrunched-up face and counted his beautiful little fingers and toes, I knew I would ALWAYS stand willing to protect him from any physical harm. I would not hesitate. I'd gladly, a thousand times over, give up my own life to protect him.

And then the realization hit me of exactly what God had done. He had a son too. He felt this way too. He wanted to protect His Son too... But He also created me – Jessie, this horribly selfish and flawed woman. And He also loved me. And being the one completely holy God, He knew there was only one way to save us both. One of us had to die. One of us had to be perfectly clean so that when death came, the other could be made acceptable to be in the presence of His holiness. It was the only way He could keep both of us, who He loved so deeply, close to

Him. He knew I wasn't up to that. He knew it would have to be His beloved, beautiful Son. He not only sent His only Son on this awful mission, but He watched every moment of His suffering. He'd have to stand strong when His only Son begged and begged not to have to go through the humiliation and horror His enemies designed for Him. He'd have to hear His beloved Son cry out in anguish and pain. He'd have to watch Him put on public display to die a slow, torturous death. He'd have to see His only Son buried and sealed in a tomb.

And as I marveled at the gift of this perfect little baby boy in my arms, I felt hot tears of inexpressible thankfulness to that Father who loved me so much. But I also struggled to understand that strength and depth of love.

How could He?! How could He do it?!?! How could He go through with it all?!

But He did – out of a depth of love for me that I could never begin to fathom. And now I could be free. Now, instead of looking at me and seeing all my ugly, putrid pile of selfish wrongs, that completely holy God could look at me and see His beautiful, beloved Son – forever bearing the scars of having died in my place, but forever whole, alive, holy in my place. All I had to do was ask!

That beautiful voice had been calling me, tugging at my heart insistently and increasingly demanding my attention. And I did ask. I received that amazing gift of complete forgiveness. For several years now, I'd been working my way forward in learning to have a relationship with God.

I realized that when the surgeon had broken the news to me of the presence of the tumor, and my response had been one of complete faith, my holy God had fulfilled my heart's greatest need. He gave me the presence of His Holy Spirit within me. I truly was not alone. And never, ever would be again!

My family had always been close. The love in each of our homes was abundantly shared with whoever was present. Prayer was a constant and calming presence, and hugs were frequent. Though my automatic emotional response to problems was to seek solitude and work it out alone, these two weeks had been completely the opposite.

During this time, my oldest sister, Jade, broke her leg. Well, to be completely accurate, her leg was broken by a pig. Each August, Jade's family spent a week at the county fair. Her kids were active in 4-H and always raised animals to show. That year, they'd raised pigs. At the end of the fair's livestock showings, the animals were sold. Jade was helping the buyer of one of the pigs get the animal into his trailer for transport home. Suddenly the huge pig turned against Jade's leg, pushing hard against it. Her leg broke near the knee.

Having a broken limb was bad enough, but the doctor was concerned. He felt the leg had fractured too easily and recommended testing. Sure enough, Jade's bone structure was found to be extremely fragile, with a severe form of osteoporosis. She was informed she had the bones of an approximately eighty-year-old woman. So she, too, was put on medications, and her life changed dramatically.

As each medical crisis occurred, the whole family sensed the need to 'circle the wagons' and join together even more. I knew without a doubt that God was deeply involved in all of this and cared for me more than I could possibly imagine. And my family would be supporting me every step of the way.

CHAPTER TEN

The very next day, I was holding on to those promises as hard as I could. Sitting in the surgeon's office with my mom, waiting for the surgeon to enter, I kept repeating those Bible verses in my mind. Anxiety and depression were on a constant merry-go-round inside me. I was edgy and fidgety while waiting for some answers.

"Hey Jessie, how's it going?" The casual greeting from the surgeon I'd worked with so many times over the past several months had me instantly relaxing. He explained to my mom and me about the tumor he'd found during the colonoscopy and showed us both, on a diagram, its location and approximate size.

"My main concern up until this point had been the growth of the tumor," he said. "It's close to obstructing the colon, and it's growing. We need to get it out of there before the colon becomes fully obstructed. That would be a whole different type of surgery with a much longer recovery period. So we want to get the tumor out as soon as possible. But the new development of blood clots in the lungs complicates things."

I understood the complications, but for my mom's sake, he went over them in detail.

"I want you to have a filter inserted before we remove the tumor, Jessie. The Inferior Vena Cava (IVC) filter will prevent further dangerous clots from entering the heart and lungs."

"Can I get that done here at this hospital?" I asked. I'd never heard of that kind of procedure being done here.

"No, unfortunately, you'll have to go to one of our affiliate hospitals that has an Interventional Radiology team. The hospital is about an hour away. It's usually an outpatient surgery and shouldn't take very long. I'll send them the order, and they'll contact you to schedule the appointment and answer any questions you may have about it. After the filter is in, we can schedule the surgery to remove the tumor."

While my mom asked several more questions, which the surgeon patiently answered, I was feeling partially relieved. The clots had worried me – a lot. I never ever wanted to feel again that panic I'd felt that night in the ED. I knew the filter was a really good decision and was anxious to have it inserted. It was a very necessary safety measure at this point. But another concern had me biting my lip and locking my body into motionless awareness. I didn't know how to get the question out, but somehow I had to. Taking a shallow breath, which was all I could seem to manage, I pushed out a single word.

"Chemotherapy?"

Though it came out barely above a whisper, the surgeon turned to me and, in a gentle voice, said, "Following the surgery to remove the tumor, I will refer you to our oncologist. He'll explain what he finds in the results of the surgery and biopsies, and will work out a treatment plan with you. But yes, I believe you are going to need to have chemotherapy. That means you'll most likely need to undergo another procedure in order to have a medi-port inserted."

It was all I could do to nod in understanding. The necessary pleasantries were exchanged as the visit with the surgeon ended, but I was barely aware of any of it.

Chemotherapy… I have to have chemotherapy…? So many questions about the future were crowding my mind! And no answers. There would be no answers for a long time. Father, hold me close! I'm so scared!

A few days later, I lay flat on my back on a surgery table at the affiliate hospital, with my head turned as far to the left as possible. Partially sedated, I could still follow commands, answer questions, and feel the dull pressure on my neck as a surgeon probed to find the correct entry point for the insertion of the filter. Thankfully, I felt nothing as the tiny opening was made, and the filter was inserted into a blood vessel and then threaded down the vessel to be secured in the correct place. The procedure went quickly and smoothly. Still halfway sleepy from the partial sedation, I was wheeled back into the room where my sister was waiting.

"Coffee?"

Jetta burst out laughing. "Of course, that would be the first word out of your mouth!" She brandished her own cup and said, "Lucky for you, their coffee is pretty decent. I'm sure they'll bring you some soon."

Sure enough, within five minutes, a nurse came in to assess my recovery and offered me something to eat. Very soon, I was halfway through my cup of coffee and digging into a delicious breakfast.

"Jetta, you have to try these blueberry pancakes. They're scrumptious!" So Jetta happily sat on the edge of the hospital bed, and we shared the rest of the breakfast while I described to Jetta what the procedure had been like.

"Weird," said Jetta. "I wonder how long you have to have that filter in."

"Not sure, but I'm guessing at least till after chemo is done since I'm on a blood thinner."

"Speaking of that, when is your oncology appointment? Is Mom going with you?"

Everything in me stilled. It was a moment before I could form an answer. It all still seemed so unreal.

"It's next Wednesday, and yes, Mom wants to go. I guess that's a good thing. I'm probably gonna need someone there taking notes and asking the questions I forget to ask. We're gonna have to work on making up a list of the questions we really need answers to."

Jetta reached over and covered my hand with her own, then almost automatically began to pray out loud. Immediately the cold clouds in my spirit dissolved.

Thank you, Father. Even in this place, You are with us.

The drive home included a stop at our favorite beach. Finding solace in the glory of God's creation, the two of us once again stood amazed at the glittering sunshine on the beautiful blue waves. Like millions of shimmering diamonds, the sun sparkles moved with the undulating waves. It was a sight we knew we'd never forget and one we both somehow knew we'd always associate with this one precious moment in time.

Jude surprised his mom and came to visit me. He stayed for five days! Oh, how I treasured those days! We laughed and talked, went to the beach, shopped, went out to eat at our favorite restaurants, and spent some time with Papa and Nana (All the grandkids called my parents Papa and Nana). It was a warm, happy time of togetherness for both of us.

I moved in with my parents the following week. Shelly's kids, Matt and his sister Linea, had agreed to pay a little rent to live in my beloved house and take care of it while I was away. They each had a large pet dog, and since my home had a big fenced-in yard, it was the perfect place for them. They were keeping my older black lab, Disney, for me too. It was a huge trade-off for me. Though I constantly longed for my independence and solitude, the relief of being cosseted and cared for by my family was tremendous. I soon settled in, and we all began preparing for the upcoming surgery to remove the tumor.

I had been in frequent contact with both of my kids and knew they were worried. My daughter Jamie flew in from Oregon, a few days before the surgery, so she could be with me before and after the operation. Jamie and I snuggled, watched movies, talked, laughed, and cried together. She joined in playing table games with Nana and me. And she spent a lot of precious time with Papa, walking, sitting on the porch swing together, and having deep conversations. As with Jude's visit, those days of connection were so very sweet.

CHAPTER ELEVEN

The day before the surgery, I was at work as usual. Toward the end of the workday, after reviewing the recheck of my blood work, the surgeon approached me. My manager was with him. *Uh oh. This can't be good. What now?*

"Jessie, I've just reviewed your labs. Your hemoglobin has dropped to a dangerous level. You need a blood transfusion. I'm thinking we should admit you to the hospital now so you can have the transfusion as soon as possible and be monitored through the night."

"Now?" I tried in vain to quickly wrap my head around this new shock.

"Have you noticed any new symptoms since your last labs? Especially an affinity to strong smells?"

Weirdly, I had. Every day I cleaned the recovery room equipment over and over again. The cleansing wipes used for this smelled strongly of rubbing alcohol. I'd always liked that smell, but now I couldn't seem to get enough of it. I'd take a new wipe out of the container and hold it up close to my nose and deeply inhale the smell very often these days. And I'd always hated cigarette smoke. But lately, I'd noticed that every time Shelly lit up a cigarette, I stayed as close to her as possible so I could breathe in that strong smell as much as possible.

I nodded and said a quiet "Yes."

My manager saw the look on my face and rightly interpreted it as reluctance – and shock. "Couldn't she just have the transfusion now and then spend the night at home? She'd rest so much better there."

The surgeon deliberated a minute, then agreed. "Alright, I'll order the transfusion now. You'll have to go to the lab, get a Type and Crossmatch done, then wait for them to get the blood ready. We'll do the transfusion down in the OB department so they can monitor you. If you do well through the transfusion, you can go home for the night. Go ahead and clock out and go straight to the lab. I'll put the orders in."

I nodded numbly. Moving mechanically, I went to the locker room, changed out of my surgical scrubs, clocked out, and went to the lab for the blood draw. Afterward, I called Jamie to tell her of the change in plans. She agreed to pick me up after the blood transfusion.

Sitting there alone as the blood was flowing in, I had a couple of hours to review all that had happened. The room was quiet, and the view of the lake was comforting. I tried not to think about all the questions and uncertainties buzzing in my mind. I couldn't answer them anyway. Knowing this could be the last time I was really alone for quite a while, I took some time to just rest in God's goodness and peace.

All too soon, the big day had arrived. August 26th. The day the tumor would be removed. Having now gone through the process of checking in for both a colonoscopy and the filter placement, I knew what to expect on the day of surgery.

"You'll be allowed to be with me in the pre-op room while they're getting me ready," I told Jamie. "They'll check me in, start the IV and draw blood, and make sure all the paperwork is filled out. Then the surgeon, the anesthesiologist, and the nurse will each come in to talk to us and make sure all our questions are answered."

"What about after surgery?" Jamie asked. "And how long will it take?"

"They'll take you to a waiting area during the surgery. Toward the end of it, they'll take you to the hospital room I'll be staying in for a few days. We'll ask the surgeon how long the operation will take."

Jamie felt a lot better after a few of my coworkers stopped in to wish me well. Seeing the closeness of the team and my complete confidence in them helped calm her anxiety a bit. The surgeon told her to expect a wait of around three hours or so. Jamie hugged and kissed me, then watched as I was wheeled away.

Three hours came and went, but Jamie received no word. She had the strange sensation that time went on and stood still at the same time. Her worry increased by the minute. As the four-hour mark approached, a nurse in surgical scrubs came out and sat down beside her. Frightened, Jamie tried to brace herself for the worst.

But the nurse smiled kindly. "The surgery is taking longer than expected as the surgeon had to do a little more than anticipated. But it's in the last stages now. The hard part is over. The tumor is out, and they're finishing up. It'll probably be less than thirty minutes now."

Jamie felt she'd faint with relief. "Thank you! Thank you so much! I was so worried!"

Within a few minutes, an aide arrived to escort Jamie to a hospital room to await my admission following the recovery period. The room's window looked out over Lake Michigan, and Jamie found her anxious spirit quieting in refreshing prayer.

But the peace was short-lived.

I was wheeled into the room, and the monitor and IV were hooked up to me. I was only semi-conscious and almost immediately went back to sleep. When I awoke again, it was to a world of pain.

"Push this button, Mom! It's pain medicine." Jamie put my hand on the button connected to the IV, and I immediately pushed the button. The pain subsided a little, and I was able to talk with her for a while. She told me about the surgery going longer than expected and how scared she was. I brushed it off and changed the subject, making a mental note to ask the surgeon about it later.

Jamie and I talked only a short time before I had to go to sleep again. My mind and body were so worn out. I relaxed into the forgetfulness of sleep with a grateful heart. Some time later, after at least one more round of visiting with Jamie and then napping, my parents arrived to take her out to dinner.

Just after they left, it happened. PAIN!!! Pain so bad I couldn't hold still. In desperation, I pushed the button for a boost of IV pain medication. But it wasn't enough. I began crying out in pain. Restlessly twisting and turning, I was in danger of tearing loose my surgical sutures.

Finally, a nurse rushed into the room. He'd heard me crying out, and seeing me writhing in the bed, he gently pressed my shoulders back into the mattress and, in a firm voice, commanded, "Jessie, look at me!"

I automatically focused on him but then immediately began to cry out in pain again.

"Jessie, you're a nurse. You need to tell me what's wrong and what you need." His firm, commanding voice reached me, and I ground the words out.

"My back!" I cried. "My back is in spasms! My back and my belly!"

I had a sledding accident when I was only 20. I'd sustained a compression fracture in my lower spine and had suffered from frequent back pain ever since. Now those muscles, having just been forced to hold still through the long surgery, were causing painful spasms with every breath. My abdominal muscles decided to join in the fun and began cramping as well. It was more pain than I'd ever known in my life.

"Ok, tell me what you need. You've dealt with this before, right? What do you need?"

As the nurse's voice penetrated my pain-wracked mind, I figured out what to say. The names and doses of the two-medication combination that had calmed this pain in the past were easy to remember. They seemed like a lifeline I longed to be able to grab hold of.

The nurse hurried off and was soon back with exactly what I had requested. As the unbearable pain began to subside, I concentrated on relaxing. And then I realized with thankfulness that Jamie had left just in time. *Thank You, God, for sparing her from that! I'm so grateful she didn't have to witness that. My poor kids have enough to deal with just knowing about all this going on with my health. Thank You for getting the pain under control before Jamie came back.*

By the time she returned, I was resting as comfortably as possible again. We were able to enjoy a little more visit time before she had to leave. Her flight back to Oregon couldn't be put off any longer.

Jamie knew she'd never forget that day. As I slept intermittently throughout the day, in between, I'd been unable to hide that my body was wracked with pain and I needed extra medication. We had great talks at times, and we'd definitely grown even closer through the experience. But for months afterward, Jamie quaked inwardly each time she remembered having to watch helplessly as her mom lay there writhing in pain. I didn't know she'd witnessed my horrible pain. I'd been only half aware at the time.

She hated having to leave just then, but she was scheduled to lead a mission team and had already missed the first week of their training in order to spend those few precious days with me and her grandparents. The airports and flights took all day. She took turns praying and sleeping all the way back.

I spent three nights in the hospital. Mom and Jetta took turns sitting with me in my room after Jamie left. As with my previous hospital stay, there were games, laughter, quiet talks, reading, and prayer times between my naps.

The first morning after surgery, a different surgeon came in to check on me. He'd assisted in the operation. I knew him well from work. He clarified for me in more technical terms the reasons for the extended surgery, knowing I'd understand and want to know. I learned that the tumor was slightly larger than a baseball and had attached itself to the wall of the abdomen. This meant more work than they had at first expected. They had also removed some adhesions, and they'd taken several lymph nodes from the area around the tumor for biopsy. I was reassured by this news. It explained the answers to several questions I'd been keeping to myself.

Later that afternoon, several of my surgery coworkers came in to visit. I found, to my embarrassment, that I was a VIP of sorts. As I'd worked in this hospital years ago and had returned last year, I was known and liked by almost everyone. Many employees stopped in to wish me well during my stay and had even taken up a collection for me! It warmed my heart and made a difficult time a little easier.

CHAPTER TWELVE

Years and years of nursing. All that learning, knowledge, and practice. All the teaching experience at so many levels. All that professionalism. All gone. It disappeared as if it had never been. Suddenly, oh so suddenly, I was just a scared patient wondering if I had a future and what that might be like. I couldn't remember it all. I couldn't teach myself. And I couldn't answer my own questions, let alone anyone else's. Being a nurse seemed like a foreign concept to me now. The professional nurse had been replaced by the scared patient, and I had no idea how or for how long.

I'm on the flip side now! Everything is all turned around!

Mom and I met with the primary surgeon for the surgery follow-up visit just four days later. The cancer had been labeled Stage 3C. He went on to explain the reasoning for the number of lymph nodes they removed and that a large number of those had come back from pathology as positive for cancer.

"I'm meeting with the cancer board this Friday to discuss your case and formulate a personalized plan going forward," he said. "You're off work for at least 6 weeks. You'll probably have the surgery to place the medi-port next week. Then you'll meet with the oncologist on September 16th to finalize your plan and start chemotherapy."

That was all I got out of that meeting. I couldn't process anymore. I was sort of aware of my mom talking with the surgeon and taking some more notes, but I couldn't listen. I felt detached. Almost like I was watching all this happen to someone else and couldn't begin to feel it. As the meeting ended and we left the building, I withdrew into myself. The sound of my mom explaining it all to my dad as he drove us home was like a distant murmur.

Ever since I'd seen the words Invasive adenocarcinoma written on that report when I was struggling for breath in the ED, I'd been an emotional wreck. It seemed like I spent every day feeling weepy and teary-eyed. My emotions were almost always just barely contained. Often, I couldn't help but let a few tears slip quietly down my face. I tried hard not to let anyone see them. My family was dealing with enough of their own grief and struggles. I wondered how in the world a person could ever go through all this without God. He was my Rock. I desperately needed Him, and He was right there with me – all the time.

For at least two weeks after surgery, the pain in my belly was knife-sharp at times. Especially in the left lower area where they'd had to remove some adhesions. Sometimes I found it hard to focus on anything, but the pain. But I strove not to show it. I knew Mom and Jetta probably saw through it, but I was determined not to be any more of a burden than I already felt like I constantly was. I confessed it all to my little journal. Opening up my heart, I let out all the things I wouldn't let myself say out loud.

It hurts! So bad! I can't focus. I don't wanna even try. I miss my kids so much. I miss my friends. I miss life being predictable. I'm so scared of the future these days. Not so much of the physical pain and changes but of the financial problems. House payments, utility payments, car payments, how much I'll have to be off work. I SO don't wanna be a burden to anyone! I know my parents want me near where they can watch over me and care for me, but they're not young, and they need their rest. And Jetta's so busy helping people who really need her, but she's devoted to helping me and being there for me too. How do I find the balance we all need??

That was the day I began writing down some scripture passages and songs I'd like included in my funeral. Weird. Maybe premature. But it was on my mind to start getting things organized. I'd always thought people who did that so early were giving up. Now I knew better. It was a way of finding some small measure of control, in a world where all the control I ever thought I had seemed to have been ripped brutally from my hands, leaving me shaky and scared.

The meeting with the oncologist was yet another emotional crisis. This one was HUGE. I felt like my whole future was on the line as Mom and I walked into the oncology wing of the hospital. This area was carpeted and quiet. The walls were pleasantly decorated with hopeful, encouraging sayings. The reception/nurses' desk where we checked in had several plaques of various sizes, also with phrases of belief, confidence, and optimism. The whole atmosphere was calm and soothing. It wasn't helping me much.

Breathe, Jessie. Breathe. You know them. They're good people and good at what they do. Don't try to hold it in. They're used to emotion here. You're not alone.

We were immediately led to a patient room. At the threshold, the warm fuzzy atmosphere stopped. This was a white-tiled, white-walled patient exam room like any other. There was the usual exam table with a clean paper liner over the vinyl top. A step-up patient scale sat against the near wall. Opposite it, facing us, were two navy blue hard plastic chairs and an over-the-bed table on wheels. In the front side corner, there was a small sink and a couple of cupboards.

The two chairs told me that here they expected patients to arrive with accompaniment. That was a minor comfort. We took off our coats and sat on the plastic chairs without talking. Thankfully the wait was brief. The aide quickly came in and measured my weight and vital signs, asked me a few questions about current medications and allergies, and clarified my surgical history. But it wasn't rushed. She took her time and really listened to my answers, taking notes as we talked.

As the aide left the room, I took a deep breath. Mom reached over and took my hand. "God's in this, Jessie. All you have to do is trust Him. He'll take care of you no matter what." Refocused by those simple words, I closed my eyes and prayed, "Father, not my will, but Yours be done. Please just get glory from this." Once again, the room filled with indescribable peace.

The oncologist entered the room carrying a computer and a file folder. He greeted us with a warm smile. After washing his hands, he came over and sat down on a rolling stool facing us, opening the file folder and spreading out some papers. Then he ignored the papers and looked from me to my mom.

Gently he said, "I imagine all of this has been a bit of a shock to you both. I'm very sorry. Cancer is a scary thing. I know you're worrying about a bunch of different things. I know you have a lot of questions. So first, let's talk about the type of cancer you have and what we need to do about it."

Again, both Mom and I immediately relaxed. He understood, at least as much as anyone without cancer could. He was friendly and approachable but also very knowledgeable. He explained that my colon cancer was a common type of cancer and was readily treatable.

"But unfortunately, that treatment does require chemotherapy."

I closed my eyes as they filled with tears. *Help me, Father. Hold me in Your arms. I'm so scared now!* I felt Mom's warm hand cover my suddenly icy ones. Compassionately, the oncologist had paused, giving me a chance to process this news and collect myself. When I felt I could breathe again, I opened my eyes and nodded to him.

"I know that's not what you wanted to hear. I'm sorry. Let me finish explaining, and then we can talk about chemotherapy."

Unable to speak, I nodded again and he continued.

"Also, unfortunately, the tumor you had was aggressive. It had invaded the wall of the colon. With its removal, the surgeons also removed several lymph nodes from the surrounding area. Those lymph nodes were tested and most of them came back cancerous. Because the cancerous tumor had gone through the colon wall and involved so many lymph nodes, we label it Stage 3C. Thankfully it had not reached Stage 4, which would have meant it had metastasized to another site."

He explained a bit further, taking his time and making sure we were understanding, and then said, "Now, let's talk about chemotherapy. First of all, you will need to have the surgery to implant the medi-port. The surgeon will implant the port in your chest and close the skin over it. Then at each chemotherapy treatment, the nurse will access the port through the skin for the chemotherapy infusion."

Mom and I listened closely as he went on to explain the options for chemotherapy. The first option he said we'd try would be to have a chemotherapy infusion once every three weeks. I would then have to take chemotherapy pills every day for two weeks, take no pills for the third week, then begin the cycle again with another infusion. He told us the names of the chemo meds, and I promptly forgot them. They were drugs I'd never heard of before, and I had no capacity for the triviality of learning about them just now.

"If you can't tolerate or react badly to the pills, we'll stop the pills and simply have you increase the frequency of infusions to once every two weeks. Almost everyone who can't tolerate the first option is able to handle the second option well. We'll give you a prescription to prevent nausea in hopes that will help you with the first option."

And then, it was time for questions.

"Will I lose my hair?" I had to smile. I had so many questions and concerns buzzing around in my head, and this was the first one to pop out? Silly vanity.

The oncologist smiled. "Your hair will thin out quite a bit, but you most likely will not lose your hair completely."

"What about work? Will I be able to keep working?"

"Well, I'd say you will be able to keep working, at least for a while. Some people are able to work all the way through chemo, but most are not. Chemotherapy tends to have a cumulative effect. You're very likely to have increasing weakness and fatigue."

I thought about that while my mom asked what side effects we'd have to watch for.

"Mostly nausea and vomiting. We don't want you to get dehydrated. Also, numbness and tingling in the hands and feet. Those are the most common difficult side effects. Oh, and you'll want to stay away from eating or drinking anything cold. Cold will likely become very painful as your nerves become more sensitive due to the chemo."

My mom took notes all the way through the meeting. When the oncologist had answered all the questions we could think of, and many we hadn't thought of, the meeting ended with instructions to make yet another appointment for surgery – this time for insertion of the medi-port.

CHAPTER THIRTEEN

I squirmed around, trying to get comfortable in my dad's big leather recliner. I was thankful the surgery to insert the port had gone smoothly, but it was more painful afterward than I'd expected. No matter what position I tried, the surgical area in the left upper part of my chest seemed to pull and ache and sting all at the same time.

I thought back to the day I'd gone to visit my best friend, Dana. Sweet, bubbly, generous Dana had to face breast cancer a couple of years ago. She'd undergone bilateral radical mastectomies – removal of both her breasts – plus infections to the surgical sites. Having finished long courses of IV chemotherapy treatments through her port, she was still taking chemotherapy pills. It seemed like it had been nightmare after nightmare for her! But when Dana heard about my diagnosis, she called me immediately.

"I'm so sorry, Jessie! I can't believe you have to go through this too." I could hear the tears in my best friend's voice and found that I, too, had tears rolling down my cheeks. Dana understood in ways my family never would. "Please come over as soon as possible. I want to help you as much as I can!"

So I went to visit Dana. That long, hard hug, so filled with shared compassion and understanding, had somehow quieted, for a few minutes, the chaos my world had become.

"I have so much to share with you!" Dana began. "There are so many things no one tells you about cancer and chemotherapy! But first, let's sit down and get comfy with some coffee. I want to hear all about what you've been through so far."

And as we snuggled together on the sofa, I poured out to her all that had happened. Dana, also a nurse, understood far more than I put into words.

"I know you're scared, Jessie. You don't have to try to hide anything from me. I'm going to be your safe person. The person you can say everything to. The person you can unload your heart to in words you won't be able to speak to your family. I know how close your family is, and I know how much you all love each other. I know they're going to want to be there for you every step of the way, and that's wonderful! Priceless! But believe me, there are going to be experiences, feelings, and thoughts you won't want or be able to share with them."

I nodded. "There already are." I hadn't felt able to pour out my fears and anxieties to my family. They knew to an extent, but they hadn't experienced it and couldn't identify with it. I now realized that Dana was right.

"I didn't even know I needed this," I confessed. "Now I'm so ashamed that I wasn't there for you more when you went through all this."

"There was no way you could have known or understood," Dana said. "You did the best you could at the time." We shared another teary hug.

Then Dana smiled. "Now let's get you some answers to questions you don't even know you're going to have."

With that, Dana had begun a list of explanations.

"First of all, what have they told you about hair loss? Will you lose your hair with your type of chemo?"

I shook my head. "No, they said it'll thin out but shouldn't fall out completely."

"Ok," said Dana, "but there's a chance of it?" At my nod, Dana picked up a pamphlet she'd saved for the past several months. "This is the best place I've found for head coverings and wigs. You have to be really picky. If you do lose all your hair, you're very likely to get painful sores on your scalp. You want some really soft, smooth head coverings on hand because it can happen very fast. Mine all fell out at once."

I looked through the pamphlet as Dana explained about thin head coverings versus wigs.

"I got a couple of really nice wigs, but I ended up only wearing them once or twice. They fit me really well and are comfortable for short periods of time, but you have to wear something smooth under them because they can hurt your scalp. Even if you don't get the sores, your scalp will feel really tender if your hair all falls out."

As Dana went on to describe her favorite thinner head coverings, she put one in my hands. "Feel how soft and smooth it is? Almost like silk or satin. This is what you want it to feel like on a tender scalp. It also doesn't seem to hurt the sores much."

The next problem Dana explained was more unexpected. "You're going to get a really dry mouth from the chemo. The stuff we sometimes use for patients actually works really well for this. Oh, what's that stuff called? Hang on a sec."

She left the room and soon brought back a familiar-looking bottle. "Just spray this in your mouth, and it'll help a lot. And it won't bother the sores."

"Sores? Sores in my mouth?"

Dana nodded sympathetically. "Yes, both dryness and sores in your mouth are pretty common with chemo. Your teeth may feel like they're all loose and going to fall out too. Don't worry, they're fine."

I took a deep breath and let out a sigh. "Ok, what's next?"

"I'm sorry. I know it's a lot..."

"Yeah, but it's stuff I really need to know. Go ahead. What's next?"

Dana hesitated, looking at me closely. Then she said, "Well, there's a bit more to losing your hair. You don't just lose it off your head. You lose ALL your hair. All over your body."

"Oh! Oh, I'd never thought about it that way... Well, then I won't hafta shave anymore." I smiled.

Dana laughed. "No, but you'll have other problems. The first few days after losing your hair, you'll wake up in the morning to a nasty surprise. No hair anywhere means no hair inside your nose. You'll sit up and snot will just run out of your nose like water."

"Eeeewwwwww!! That sounds messy. So a box of tissues beside the bed."

"Yeah, you'll go through a lot of those. Keep some in your purse and car too. You'll also lose eyelashes and eyebrows."

My thick, dark eyebrows went up in surprise. "Oh, I never thought of that!"

"I know," Dana grunted. "It sure caught me by surprise. You don't realize how much dirt and gunk your eyelashes protect your eyes from until they're not there anymore."

"Wow, your eyes must get really irritated then." I tried to picture myself without eyebrows and eyelashes and couldn't.

"Exactly," Dana said, "so you'll want to keep Liquid Tears eye drops with you all the time."

Then Dana picked up another small bottle. "This is a liquid eyebrow. It looks more like real eyebrows than anything else I've found." On her own forearm, she showed me how to apply the eyebrow makeup, shaping and feathering it out to look like a real eyebrow.

And just like that, it suddenly hit me hard... Dana, my best friend, had to face all these awful surprises and figure out how to handle them all by herself! I hung my head, and tears once again filled my eyes.

"What's wrong?" Dana came closer and put her arm around me. "What is it?"

"I've been such a horrible friend to you! I had no idea about any of this! And you had to do it all alone! I'm so sorry. I SO wish I'd understood better and been here for you more." The tears of remorse spilled down my cheeks. This load must have been so incredibly heavy for Dana to bear!

But she put her fingertips under my chin, tipping my head up so she could look into my eyes. "I'm so thankful you didn't know, Jessie. I hoped you'd never know. Because you knowing and really understanding would have meant that you'd had to face it all too. I would give just about anything to protect you from all this. I'm only glad I already learned it all so I can help you through it."

Stunned, I hugged her tightly and then said, "I guess I'm beginning to understand what you mean by that. Unless you've gone down this road yourself, you can't truly get it."

Dana smiled again. "But now we'll be closer friends than ever. We'll share this journey together. We'll be there for each other in ways we never could have before."

I sighed through the tears. "Thank you, God, for this amazing friend you've given me!"

Finally, I squared my shoulders. "Ok, next?"

"Well, that's most of the physical stuff. You're obviously aware your emotions are becoming more extreme. That roller coaster isn't going to stop, but you will get used to it – kinda. You'll have pain, though. Pain you can't explain. Especially in your hands and feet, but it'll happen all over. Nerve pain. Did they give you prescriptions for pain and nausea?"

"Yes, I have those filled and ready."

"Good," Dana said, "how about for anxiety?"

I shook my head. "No, they had to give me Valium in the hospital for back spasms, but other than that, I haven't really been anxious."

"Call and ask for a prescription for something for anxiety and make sure it's something you're allowed to take before your first few chemo infusions. It will make that dreadful experience a bit easier."

"Oh. Ok. That makes a lot of sense. Yikes, this is crazy." I felt my head swimming with it all.

"I know. It's a scary new world, isn't it? I promise I'll be here and help as much as I can." Dana looked closely at me again. "There's only a little more we need to go over today."

I nodded, signaling I was ready.

"You need a chemo bag," Dana said. "You're going to need to bring some specific things with you to your chemo infusions." She picked up a knit bag by her feet. "In this, I keep the little binder they give you for recording all your medications, any side effects you experience, all your lab values, all the oncology contact information, etc." She showed me the little binder; the two of us went through it together, page by page. "They'll give you one before your first infusion, and they'll want you to bring it every time."

"Ok, do I have to remember all that stuff?" I was overwhelmed by the amount of specific information the binder contained.

"No, they'll fill in most of it. You just hand it to them at the beginning of your infusion, and they write it all in. All you really have to keep track of is your medications and any side effects. Record any and all side effects, even simple things like a headache. It's all important."

I nodded again, and Dana went on.

"There are also a few other things you'll need at infusions. Get yourself a warm, soft and cozy throw blanket. Make sure it's thick and snuggly and long enough to cover you from the neck down. You're on a strong blood thinner, and you'll definitely get cold at infusions. The big recliners they have for patients are heated and powered, so no effort involved to lay back. You'll almost certainly fall asleep during the infusion. I always do."

"Yeah, with these clots in my lungs, I get tired really easily, and I haven't even started chemo yet."

Dana nodded. "Yup, you'll definitely need the rest there. Be sure to pack a book to read, some Vernors at room temp, and some crackers. Trust me, that's what helps most with nausea. They'll load your infusions with anti-nausea medication, but you'll still feel pretty icky."

She paused, then picked up a small white binder with two words written in large, flowing script on the front of it, 'You Can...'. "I got this for you," she said, handing it over.

I opened the front cover to find it was a journal with blank, lined pages. I looked up at Dana with questions in my eyes.

"Keep this with you," Dana said. "There will be times, even during infusions with your family sitting by your side or sitting at home resting, when you desperately need to just let it all out. You'll have things to say that you'd never say to your family. Things that might hurt them if they knew you were experiencing it. You might suddenly need to dump a bunch of anger that's not directed at anybody but at this journey in general. I can't explain it better than that. You'll know what to write and when. I do suggest that in the very front of it, you write out all the dates and times and specifics of all that's happened so far. You're going to want a record of it all someplace. Obviously, you'll want to explain to your family that this is your private journal."

Again I nodded in wordless understanding. I'd already experienced some of what Dana was describing, and though I'd never been good at journaling, I knew this would be far different. I already knew the gist of what some of the entries in this journal would contain.

"Other than that, you'll want to keep in here some hand sanitizer, some tissues, and anything else you decide you want with you at infusions. Oh! And some warm, thick, fuzzy socks with grip spots on the soles. You'll definitely want those!"

I couldn't thank my friend enough as we said our goodbyes – once again, tearfully hugging and saying a prayer for each other.

One other thing Dana had given me that day was what she called a 'port pillow'. It was a small, fluffy pillow she'd sewn together and attached a Velcro ring on the back of.

"Put it around your seatbelt in the car," Dana said, "right where the seat belt goes over your port. It'll help it not to hurt so much." I had used it on the way home from the hospital after surgery and found that Dana was right again.

Now, as I struggled to get comfortable, I remembered that it was Dana who had also suggested sleeping in the recliner for a couple of nights after getting the port put in so gravity wouldn't pull on it so much and it'd hurt less. As the pain medication finally kicked in and I settled down to sleep, I thanked God over and over again for such a wonderful friend.

CHAPTER FOURTEEN

CHEMOTHERAPY...

One of the scariest words ever. At least for me. But it was something that happened to other people, and I could just be sympathetic and as understanding as possible – and keep that nice, safe wall up that distanced me from all that went with that word.

Until today. September 16th.

The day I had to watch and endure as that wall crumbled to pieces.

Somehow, even with all the doctor appointments and surgical procedures and hospitalizations, in my mind, this day had been relegated to a distant future of 'Someday'.

'Someday' wasn't ever supposed to actually arrive...

But it was far, far worse than that.

It wasn't just that the luxury of 'Someday' suddenly disappeared. As my wall of perceived safety disintegrated in front of me, I now had to walk right through the rubble left by that wall and face what was waiting on the other side. No more distancing myself. No more pretending to understand while not really wanting to. No more hiding.

Turns out a lot of people do that. There's something about the word 'cancer' that really scares people, even when it happens to someone else. But when it happened to me, I began to notice something. A strange shift takes place. Suddenly, people I'd known for many years began to disappear. They just dropped out. I stopped hearing from them and even stopped coincidentally running into them in public places. They suddenly just weren't around anymore. On the flip side of that, people I hadn't heard from since high school and even earlier came out of the woodwork. I heard from many I'd known well all those years ago but hadn't stayed close to because our lives had gone in different directions. One high school friend, in particular, sent me a package of things to do during chemo treatments or times when I was too weak to do anything else. She also began to frequently send me personal cards of encouragement, and she kept it up all the way through.

Cancer has so many weird twists and turns like that. In so many ways, it flips around what you've become familiar with until you hardly recognize your world.

I got up that morning and immediately felt anxiety churning in my belly. Mechanically, I pushed myself through getting ready for this oh-so-difficult day. Dana had instructed me on how to dress for it. Warm, loose, comfortable clothing with a V-neck or button-up shirt so the port would be easy to access without much exposure. My 'chemo bag' was all packed and ready to go according to the list Dana gave me. Physically, I was as ready as I could be.

But mentally?? Emotionally?? Not even close.

As soon as I saw my mom that morning, I knew I wasn't alone. Mom was going through a lot of the same feelings I was. And poor Dad! He was trying so hard to be strong! I realized then that whether you're the patient or the family, chemotherapy isn't something you could ever really be ready for. You can prepare as much as possible, and still it's incredibly hard!

Dad drove Mom and me to the hospital. Dana had warned me that I would be weak and sleepy and not feeling too great after the infusion, so they knew I wouldn't be up to driving home by myself.

Mom and I walked silently down the long hallway to the oncology department. We had to meet with the oncology Nurse Practitioner for approximately thirty minutes before going to the infusion center. This was the easy part. Vital signs, weight, assessment of the tumor removal site and the port insertion site, assessment of lungs, assessment of current symptoms, review of lab results, review of symptoms to watch for... all routine stuff. We had already attended a meeting there for the 'Chemo Teach' session to inform us of what to expect.

Now the Nurse Practitioner led us through a review of the chemotherapy treatment plan. As both Dana and the oncologist had advised, I arranged to take the following day off as a recovery day. This was to be the tentative plan for treatment and recovery over the next few months. I had already discussed it with my manager, who had readily agreed.

As the pre-infusion appointment came to an end, I found I wanted to beg for more time to prepare. Another day or two to somehow wrap my head around it all. Maybe after the weekend, I'd be able to face it.

But I held it in. I fought the panic and made myself go on.

Mom and I left the oncology department, walked back down the long hallway to the main entrance, and then the short hallway to the Infusion Center. Just outside the door, we stopped and looked at each other. Then, taking a deep breath to steady myself, I walked through the door.

While checking in at the reception desk, we looked around. There was a curved line of recliners separated by partitioning curtains. All the recliners were positioned to face a huge window that curved around this section of the hospital and looked out over Lake Michigan. The waves of the lake rolled up onto a shoreline just a few yards away. It was a gorgeous view!

We were led to one of the recliner cubicles and found there was a separate cushioned chair for visitors there. It was comforting to know that visitors were not only welcomed but expected here. I couldn't imagine facing this alone.

The material of the recliner was cold, and I hurriedly pressed the heating button on the table attached to the armrest. I was nervous and fidgeting. And I was so scared! But I was trying not to show it because I knew Mom was scared too. A knot of anxious dread formed in my stomach, and my limbs felt like jelly.

Then God showed His amazing mercy again. A familiar face peeked around the curtain, then the nurse walked over to me. It was Bree. I had known and worked with her for years but hadn't seen her in a while. As I raised my frightened eyes, I met the calm, comforting understanding in Bree's. I felt some of my anxiety begin to fade.

"It's gonna be ok, Jessie," Bree said. "I know this is all new to you, and you're scared. I'm so sorry you have to go through this! I was shocked when I saw your name on the patient list. I read your chart. Wow, this must have been a brutal month for you!"

I gave a half-hearted smile. "Yeah, it hasn't exactly been fun."

Bree smiled warmly. "Well, I'm going to take good care of you. First, let's start with a couple of heated blankets and get you comfortable. I'll be right back." And as she almost immediately returned and tucked me in with heated blankets, covering me from shoulders to feet, I breathed a sigh of relief. I felt some of the tension begin to ease out of my shoulders, and the icy ball of fear in my stomach began to melt a little. I chatted easily with Bree as my vital signs were measured and my symptoms were clarified.

"Now…" Bree looked me in the eye and asked, "Has your port been accessed since it was put in?"

"No," I answered, "every doctor just assesses the insertion site every time they see me."

Bree nodded. "I'm not surprised. Everything has happened really fast in your case. Ok, then, that's our first step. I'm going to access it and flush it, then leave the needle and tubing in so we can get your treatment started. Did they give you numbing cream for the site?"

"Yes, I put it on with the clear dressing about half an hour ago."

"Ok, good. I'll clean that off now and get the supplies to access your port. I'll be right back."

I could only nod. The anxiety suddenly returned, full force. *Here it comes. This is the beginning. I wonder what the end will look like.* I looked over at my mom, sitting quietly in her semi-comfortable padded visitor's chair. Seeing my own anxiety mirrored there, I nevertheless also saw peace.

"How are you doing?" Mom was watching me closely.

I shrugged and dropped my eyes. "You know what surprises me? Even being a nurse and knowing exactly what steps have to be taken and the complete mechanics of everything that they're going to do doesn't help. I'm so hugely anxious and scared. I wanna run away and never come back. And I can't. I can't. I have to go through this."

I looked back up at my mom. "Thank you again for being here with me, Mom. I'm not alone. Jesus is here with us, and His peace will help us." And then, quoting one of my favorite hymns I said, "When trials like sea billows roll... It is well with my soul."

With tears in her eyes, Mom said, "Yes! Trust Him, Jessie. He's here, and He's not going to let go of you."

Bree returned and cleansed the numbing cream off my port area. Then, taking the over-the-bed table on wheels that was beside my chair, began to lay out the necessary sterile equipment. As she worked, she explained, "Your chemotherapy infusion has been ordered. But it depends on your lab results, and we have to wait until you arrive each time to process the order so the pharmacy can deliver it here to the Infusion Center." Finished with the set-up, she put on a mask and asked me to expose my port site again. With trembling fingers, I stretched the open collar of my 'chemo shirt' wide and held it like that. Bree put on sterile gloves and began to swab the skin over and around the port area with a strong cleansing agent.

I shivered as the cold swab rubbed across my skin. Bree finished swabbing and began getting the needle and tubing ready as she waited for my skin to dry. When it was time, Bree touched her gloved fingers to the skin over my implanted port, feeling for the correct placement of the needle and holding the port between her thumb and finger.

"Now, when I tell you, take a deep breath, and I'll insert the needle. The deep breath pushes the port out toward me and makes it easier. Ok?"

"Yeah."

"Ok, here we go. I'll count to three, then tell you to take a deep breath. One, two, three. Now take a deep breath."

I obeyed and watched as Bree expertly inserted the needle through my skin and into my port. The pain was sharp, but I had expected that and found it uncomfortable but bearable. There was a syringe already attached to the short piece of tubing, and Bree warned me I'd feel some pressure as she flushed sterile saline from the syringe through the tubing, needle, and port. She positioned the needle and its attached tubing, then applied a large sterile, see-through covering over the whole needle area, leaving the tubing hanging out so it was easily accessible.

When she was finished, Bree excused herself to go see if my chemotherapy infusion had arrived yet. Grateful for this tiny break to catch my shortened breath, I leaned my head back and closed my eyes. Taking deep breaths, I tried to calm myself, but I couldn't block out the feeling of that needle in my left upper chest.

Over the next few minutes, while we waited for my infusion to be delivered, Bree tried to make my mom and I as comfortable as possible with drinks and conversation. She brought some cold Sprite for Mom, but some room-temperature ginger ale for me, as anything cold was about to become unbearable. She also brought a few soft, cozy blankets and let me pick out my favorite.

"These are made for cancer patients by some ladies in the community. You picked my favorite! It will help keep you warm. Cold is not going to be your friend this winter. It's hard that you're starting this type of chemo at the beginning of the cold season."

Then, because I asked, Bree began to share a little of what was going on in her family life, and I, in turn, filled Bree in on the changes in my own life.

When the infusion arrived, it was in two parts. Bree explained that I needed to have some very strong anti-nausea medication and fluids infused before receiving the chemotherapy medicine. I felt the icy ball in my stomach tighten again as Bree brought the equipment to begin the first part of the infusion. She double-checked the IV bag label against my ID band and against the order. I watched as she primed the IV tubing and then hooked it to the tubing attached to the needle in my port. Bree pushed several buttons on the IV machine, setting the rate for the medication to be infused. Then she pushed the Start button.

I watched as the anti-nausea fluid began to flow through the tubing and, for my mom's sake, tried to control my face as my mind spun.

Mom reached over and took my hand. She was not fooled. She knew me far too well. Besides, she was feeling and thinking many of the same things herself. For the next half hour, we found very little to say. But we were together. Together we'd face it. Together we'd get through it. Mom quietly said a brief prayer, and amazingly it happened again. Right there in the Infusion Center, with chemotherapy about to run through my body, I felt the awesome peace of God settle over me. I finally began to relax.

The loud beeping of the IV machine startled me. Bree soon appeared again, this time gowned and masked and with special gloves on. She was carrying a different IV bag filled with a yellow fluid. The bag was inside a brown plastic bag.

"This is the chemotherapy medicine," she said. "It will take about two-and-a-half hours to run in. When it's done, we'll finish up with some more anti-nausea medicine and fluids to keep you hydrated." Hanging the chemo bag up, she again double-checked the medicine label against my ID band and the doctor's order. Then she pulled the brown plastic covering back down over the IV bag, primed the tubing, and hooked it up as she had the previous one. "Please let me know right away if you have any nausea or any other symptoms. We'll start slowly for the first half hour, then speed it up a little if you're handling it well."

Again, for what seemed like the thousandth time, I could only nod. I watched that yellow fluid begin to enter my body. I wondered, also for what seemed like the thousandth time, just how bad it would be.

This is it! All of a sudden, it's REAL!! It's time. I'd rather face almost any other three words than these… But I can't delude myself or put it off any longer. Chemo is actually starting right now! I have to face it. I have to say it.

"*I HAVE CANCER.*"

Still staring at the tubing, I heard the whispered words coming from my own mouth. They echoed as if from a long distance, but I felt them to my core. It was several seconds before I could look at my mom. When I finally did, I saw the awful truth had dawned on her too. Needing to get this moment behind us, we both took deep breaths and let them out slowly.

After that, Mom and I passed the time playing Scrabble, between my frequent trips to the bathroom, with my IV pole in tow, because of all the fluids. Occasionally, Bree would stop by to check on us and chatted for a while if she was able. I got hungry and gladly ate the bologna sandwich Mom had brought for me. We talked off and on, but after a while, I got sleepy. Bree tucked me in with a freshly warmed blanket, and I was soon sound asleep.

I awoke to Bree disconnecting the IV tubing. The chemo infusion, followed by the anti-nausea infusion, had finished. She warned me before flushing the heparin through at the end. I was glad she did. I'd given this same warning to many patients myself but hadn't really thought about it for this. Many people can taste the heparin as it gets flushed through. I was no exception. It's an awful taste, and even as I write this, the memory of it brings back the sick feeling I always felt at the end of a chemo treatment.

The taste of having cancer. The taste of sickness and fear.

I took another deep breath as Bree pulled the needle out of my port, swabbed the area, then covered it with a Band-Aid. It was over. I'd made it through the first treatment!

I felt a little lightheaded and unsteady as we stood and gathered our things, preparing to leave for home. Bree said that was normal as my body began to try to adjust to the chemo medicine. Mom and I thanked Bree warmly, then I held Mom's arm as we walked slowly down the hallway and out the front entrance. Dad was already waiting there and helped me into the front seat, then got Mom settled into the back seat. I was so tired and groggy, I just wanted to lie down and go back to sleep.

We were about a third of the way home when I suddenly sat up straight.

"Pull over, Dad! Hurry!"

He barely got the car stopped before I was out and bent over, hands pressing my sore abdomen as I retched. It was quickly over, and Dad helped me back into the car.

"So much for the bologna sandwich idea," I quipped. The rest of the trip home seemed to take forever, even though I felt so groggy. The nausea came in waves, though not as badly.

Back at my parents' house, I sank exhausted into my recliner, pulled a blanket partially over myself, and fell asleep again while Mom was still tucking the blanket more securely around me.

I was awakened by the smell of the food my parents had cooked.

"Do you want to try to eat something, honey?" Mom's voice sounded hopeful but hesitant.

"No, thanks," I managed. I closed my eyes again and drifted in and out of awareness for a while. The 'Jeopardy' theme brought my eyes open, and I stayed awake through the half-hour show. My parents watched it every weekday evening. They never seemed to get tired of it.

After the show, I talked with my parents for a little bit, then said goodnight. As I climbed the stairs to 'my' room, I thought about the day. *I guess it could have been a lot worse. Thank you, God.*

CHAPTER FIFTEEN

I slept only intermittently that night. My whole body felt heavy and abused and tired, but I also felt slightly sick to my stomach. I got up around 8 am. Knowing I wasn't up to a shower yet; I slowly made my way downstairs in my sweatshirt and pajama pants.

Mom met me in the dining room.

"Good morning, Baby. How are you feeling? Did you sleep well?" She was looking at me closely.

"Good morning. Yeah, I slept ok. I think I'm actually a little hungry."

"Good! What would you like?"

"Oh, don't bother about me, Mom. I'm just gonna try a piece of toast. You go ahead and finish getting ready."

My parents were leaving this morning to go downstate for the day to visit some family.

"Ok, let me know if you need anything."

Mom went to curl her hair while I got out a piece of bread and put it in the toaster. When it was done, I buttered it lightly and sprinkled a little cinnamon sugar over it, then took a bite. I wasn't too sure about this, but I still felt more hungry than nauseated, so I took a second bite.

It was too much too soon. Hurrying to the bathroom, I barely made it before the retching started. This time it didn't end quickly. In fact, it didn't end at all! I vomited over and over again, only getting to pause for about thirty seconds between bouts of it.

My parents were worried, but I assured them I'd be over it soon and would be fine just resting. With obvious worry and misgivings, they left a few minutes later with instructions for me to call Jetta if I needed anything.

Thankfully, I'd brought my cell phone downstairs with me. I called Jetta, but couldn't speak well between the frequent bouts of vomiting.

Jetta came over and let herself into the house.

"Jessie, this isn't good! What can I do?"

"Call the Infusion Center," I barely managed to say.

Jetta looked all over for the phone number, and with grunted instructions from me, was finally able to call. Bree was there and told Jetta to bring me in right away.

Les, Bill, Jetta and I had all worked on the local EMS service and knew all the ambulance crew members well. Now Jetta called her friend Margie, who had recently taken over their friend Sam's role as EMS Director, and explained the situation.

"Sam's wife just went through this last week," Margie said. "Let's see what they did about it."

Jetta hurriedly called Sam, who came right over. Sam and Jetta loaded me onto an ambulance cot and took me to the hospital.

I thought we'd never get there. More than once, I gave into the weakness of my spirit and cried out, "God, I can't do this! If this is how it's going to be, then please just take me home now!"

Sam was very upset by this.

"I know you, Jessie. I know you. You're stronger than that!"

When we finally reached the hospital, they wheeled me on the cot right to the Infusion Center, where Bree was waiting for us. She got me settled in a recliner and quickly accessed my port. Having already contacted the oncologist and obtained orders, she then quickly administered anti-nausea medication, then began an infusion. Jetta stayed with me while Sam took the ambulance back to town.

By this time, I had been vomiting for three hours. It took the medication some time to begin working. I kept wanting to apologize to everyone around me, but I could hardly get three words out at a time.

That was a **VERY** long day. After a few hours of receiving medications and fluids in the Infusion Center until the vomiting finally stopped, Jetta and I had to go check in at the ED. Since I was receiving treatment in the hospital, I had to be evaluated by a doctor before leaving for home. This meant a full evaluation in the busy ED.

Assessments were made, blood was drawn, more fluid was pumped into me via IV, a consult call was made to the oncologist, and a lot of waiting had to happen as the ED doctor had many patients to see. Finally, about nine hours after we'd arrived at the hospital, Bill picked up us two exhausted sisters, and drove us home. Our parents helped me into the house and got me settled into bed. I slept the night through for the first time in a long time.

I had to miss a whole day of taking the chemo pills due to the vomiting. But when the ED doctor called to consult the oncologist, the oncologist instructed that I start them the next morning. So, when I got up, I took the pills but didn't eat breakfast. My stomach had to rest. I ate nothing all that day or the next.

Finally, three days after my first chemo infusion, I tentatively ate a few bites of toast. I kept it down, but it took literally half the day to eat half a piece.

The next day I had a bit more. Slowly, over the next three weeks, I became able to eat again.

And then it was time for another oncology appointment, followed immediately by another chemo infusion. The oncologist reviewed my lab results and then brought up the very question I most needed answering.

"Well, it seems you didn't respond all that well to the first option of treatment. It sounds like you had a really rough time of it. I'm sorry. If it's ok with you, I think it might be time to switch to the second option of treatment."

"Is that easier to handle?"

I had my doubts. The long, horrible day of vomiting, with a belly still sore from surgery, made me very reluctant to continue.

"Yes and no," he said. "It means not taking the pills, but then the infusions need to be more frequent. The pills are most likely what nauseated you so badly, so that should help a lot. The second option is infusions only, but that means we need to increase the frequency to every other week instead of every third week."

"Ok, I guess that's the way to go. I hope you're right about it being the pills causing the nausea. It was really bad! I don't ever want to go through that again."

"I'm sure the pills are the culprit. They almost always are. Now, you need to know that because we're getting rid of the pills, that means that after today's infusion, we'll be changing the amount that needs to be infused. It will increase significantly. We won't be able to get the whole amount of medication into you within the afternoon of your next infusion. One of the chemo medications will finish in that amount of time, but the other one takes a lot longer. We'll need to leave the needle in your port overnight and send you home with a bag to carry the rest of the infusion medication in. It will look like a small football, and it will infuse all by itself. We'll secure the tubing to your body and give you a pouch to carry the 'football' in. Since your infusions are on Thursday afternoons, you'll need to carry your 'football' until Saturday mornings."

So the decision was made, and the oncologist changed my chemo order. This second infusion would be just like the last one, except with more nausea medication. I wouldn't have to take the 'football' home with me until next time.

But no matter what anybody said, I couldn't stop worrying about it. Dread filled my whole being as I walked into the Infusion Center with Jetta at my side.

Bree greeted us like long-lost friends and ushered us to the recliner at the far end of the line. Looking at me and seeing my tension and reluctance, Bree said, "I don't blame you for being scared, Jessie. We're going to take it slow. We've changed your combination of medications so the anti-nausea part is stronger. I think you'll find this treatment regimen a lot easier to handle."

I had been trying to talk myself into this all day. I didn't want to even try to face this second chemo treatment after that awful day of vomiting following the first treatment. My poor body had been through so much in the past month! I was tired of all the new medical problems. I was tired of facing new medical issues. I just wanted it all to go away.

And it wasn't all just physical. I was an introvert. I liked being present quietly in the background, doing whatever needed to be done without any fanfare.

That was impossible now. Everywhere I went, people stopped me to ask how I was doing and wanted to hear the whole story. It was all so big and exhausting!

But I said none of this to Bree. I said none of it to anyone. Quietly, I submitted to the measurement of my vital signs and answered Bree's questions about side effects and symptoms. Since the vomiting day, my only symptoms had been fatigue alongside intermittent nausea.

"Your blood pressure is a bit high, but I guess that's to be expected right now."

I saw the kindness and understanding in Bree's eyes, and some of my stiff resistance began to ease.

"What is it?"

"It's 156/98, and your pulse is 94. Not in danger range, but we'll check them again at the end of your treatment just in case. I'm sure it's your anxiety causing it, though." Bree smiled kindly at me.

"You can do this, Jessie. I've given these treatments to a lot of cancer patients, and seen the difference. I'm confident you'll find this regimen a lot easier to handle."

I took a deep breath and forced my shoulders to relax. It seemed like I had to do that a lot these days.

"Thank you, Bree. I really needed to hear that. I'm ready whenever you are."

Bree smiled. "Great. Let's get your port accessed and get the anti-nausea infusion started. I'll be right back."

As us two sisters waited for Bree to come back with the sterile equipment, Jetta took my cold hands in her own warm hands and prayed out loud.

"Father God, thank You that You are here with us. We love You, and we trust You no matter what. Thank You for sending Bree to help us again today. Thank You that You never stop taking care of us."

After that, everything went smoothly. Bree quickly accessed my port as before and got the fluids running. Jetta and I chatted with Bree and played games, then, when I got sleepy and snuggled down to rest, Jetta read her book until the infusion was finished.

Bree gently woke me and removed the needle from my chest, and applied a Band-Aid over the site. Jetta helped me put my coat on and carried the chemo bag as we walked out to her van. The ride home was uneventful, and I fell asleep again in my recliner as soon as we got home to our parents' house.

We all dreaded the next day. I laid awake the morning after the infusion, trying to convince myself it was okay to get up. Slowly, then, I sat up on the side of the bed. I thought through every move before I made it. I decided what clothes to wear before I stood up. Carefully I made my way to the bathroom and took my time getting ready for the day.

By the time I'd finished and got downstairs to my recliner, I was so tired, I decided to just rest there for a while. I worked the lever to raise my feet, then leaned my head back and closed my eyes.

Wow, I'm SO tired! God, bless whoever invented the recliner. Is it gonna be like this every time? I feel so completely icky. I don't even want a cup of coffee! And no way am I gonna eat anything. I guess this is one way to lose weight.

I had to smile at that thought. This weight loss plan wasn't in anybody's advertisements.

Mom gave me a cheerful, "Good morning! Did you sleep well?" And then immediately followed with, "How do you feel this morning? Any nausea?"

As moms do, she came over and put her hand on my arm, looking at me closely.

"Good morning, Mom. Yeah, I slept okay. I'm having constant mild nausea, so I'm not gonna have any breakfast."

"Do you want some coffee? Dad just made a fresh pot."

I shook my head. "No, I'm not ready for anything yet. I'm just tired. I'm gonna rest and spend some time with Jesus."

"Ok, that's probably best. I'll be nearby. Let me know if you need anything."

Mom watched as I once again laid my head back and closed my eyes, then she went off to do some housework. I knew Mom was feeling the need to mother and protect me, but also trying hard not to hover too closely. The whole family knew my need for independence and personal space. But they all wanted to help and be there for me too. It was going to be a learning process for all of us.

I settled in and cozied up with a soft blanket. Thankfully, I'd left my Bible beside my recliner. I reached over and picked it up. Sitting there quietly, I just enjoyed holding it for a few moments. I truly loved this Book. It never ceased to amaze me how God had packed centuries of human living into one big story of His love.

As I opened the beloved Bible, I automatically turned first to the Book of Isaiah. Years ago, my sister Jetta had written this verse on a notecard that I kept as a bookmark on its appropriate reference page in the Bible. This morning I read it once again.

"Yet the LORD longs to be gracious to you; He rises to show you compassion. For the LORD is a God of justice. Blessed are all who wait for Him!" Isaiah 30:18

What an amazing bunch of promises this one verse held! Reflecting once again on those promises, I went on to read passages from several other books of Scripture.

When the fatigue began to take over, I closed the Bible and leaned my head back. Peace settled over my mind and heart. Closing my eyes, I prayed until I fell asleep.

When I awoke, my parents were getting ready to have lunch. They asked if I was up to eating, and I said, "No, thanks." The thought of food was still repulsive to me. I felt the nausea kick up a notch because of the smells coming from the dining room. Holding as still as possible, I opened a game on my phone to distract myself.

Jetta arrived as my parents were finishing lunch.

"How's my favorite patient?"

"I'm not a patient today. Just a sicky," I answered.

Jetta frowned. "How bad is the nausea?"

"Eh, manageable as long as I hold pretty still. What are you up to today?"

Jetta launched into a list of all she hoped to accomplish, and I tried to pay attention. Jetta was very active in ministry through our church. Her husband, Bill, was our pastor. Jetta led a 'GriefShare' group for those who had lost a loved one, co-led a ladies' Bible study every Monday morning, participated with Bill in a small group meeting on Tuesday evenings, led the teens' Sunday school class, and also led the youth group on Wednesday evenings.

Between all those, she provided rides to doctor appointments, visited people in the hospital, spent hours on the phone with people in need, and met with people for prayer and connection all throughout the week.

Just thinking about Jetta's day made me more tired. And now she had added being there for me as much as possible. But despite that long list of ministry needs Jetta worked to meet, I knew Jetta would never, ever see me or anyone else as just a responsibility. She truly loved all the people she ministered to.

Us two girls talked for a while, but of course, I was soon tired. Jetta tucked me in, promised to stop by to see me later that evening, then left for her busy day of loving others.

After a couple of days, I finally felt I could stop worrying about having a repeat of that horrible day of vomiting, and I began to relax. Somehow, the ever-present nausea seemed to decrease day by day. It never fully went away, but after about five days, I began to eat again – little bits at first, gradually working up to a full meal.

CHAPTER SIXTEEN

Several days later, I was helping to set the table for dinner one evening. I was talking with Mom about her day as I reached into the silverware drawer. Suddenly I gave a sharp cry.

"Aaahhh! Ouch! Oh that hurt!"

The butter knife I'd grabbed clattered to the floor.

"Jessie, what's wrong?" Mom was instantly at my side, and Dad came hurrying in from the dining room.

"What happened? Jessie, are you ok?"

I was staring at my hands. Finally, I looked up into the worried faces of my parents.

"I'm sorry," I said. "They said I wouldn't be able to handle cold at all, but I never thought it'd be like this. The second I picked up the knife, it was like sharp electric shocks shooting through my hands. It hurt so bad! I didn't expect it."

After a second or two of surprise, my parents both hugged me with relief, and Dad smiled.

"Oh I'm glad that's all. You had me scared there for a minute. Ok, no handling metal silverware. We can do that."

Then, seeing my downcast face, he lifted my chin so he could see my tear-filled eyes.

"It's going to be ok, Jessie. It's a learning process. But we're all in this together. We'll all learn, and we'll all adjust together."

I nodded silently. I couldn't tell them how scared I was. I couldn't tell them how useless it made me feel. I couldn't help with the cooking because the smells were intolerable. I didn't have the stamina to do much cleaning. And now I wasn't even able to set the table? I felt so ashamed.

I waited a few moments, then slipped off to the bathroom while my parents worked on the final preparations for dinner. I shut the door and leaned back against it. Closing my eyes, I allowed the tears to fall. The fear and shame were unbearable. But I knew this was not the time or place to try to deal with them.

Taking a few deep breaths, I forced myself to calm down and shoved those reactions deep down inside me. Running water until I was sure it was warm, I splashed some on my face, then patted it dry with the hand towel. Staring in the mirror, I composed my face into a relaxed smile, then went out to join my parents. As we joined hands and Dad prayed over the meal, I silently cried out to God for help.

That night I cried myself to sleep. Alone in my upstairs bedroom, I didn't have to hide anything. So much shame. So much fear. I was only two treatments in and already unable to do simple things I'd always taken for granted. How helpless was I going to become?

The tears seemed to have no end. Facing the fear of what the pain would grow into through the cold of a northern Michigan winter made me feel small and vulnerable. If picking up a butter knife – a knife that was always in a warm house – was too much, then how was I ever going to even go outside, much less do things like clean the snow off my car after work?

Nevertheless, life was gradually falling into a routine. My oncologist and I had gotten my schedule all arranged with my supervisor. Everyone agreed I needed to have the days off immediately after an infusion for some recuperation time.

The heaviest schedules for surgery and recovery days were typically early in the week. So, beginning with the first infusion, and adjusting for the changes made starting with the third infusion, I would have my infusions on Thursday afternoons. That way, I could take Friday off and have three days of recuperation before having to work again on Monday. Every other Thursday, I'd work through the morning, then leave at lunchtime and go to my infusion. This was the schedule for as long as this worked for me.

Both my supervisor and the oncologist were adamant that I should not hesitate to inform them if and when I could no longer keep up with this timing. The thought was dreadful to me, and I vowed to keep working as long as I possibly could.

Returning to work that Monday, I found to my surprise that my coworkers had become very protective of me. No longer was I expected to take the patient's bed to the surgical room, assist in moving the patient onto the bed and then guide the heavy bed to the recovery room.

Instead, my coworkers told me to just wait in the recovery room, and they'd bring the patient to me. What a relief that was! No more physically moving the heavy beds around or lifting and moving patients. I got to just take care of them in the recovery room. Sometimes there was a brief lull between recovery patients, and I got to just sit and rest for a few minutes. It was wonderful.

And people went out of their way to check on me. They asked me how I was doing, and listened attentively to my answers. They asked about my treatments and what it was like for me. I felt so loved and cared for.

The day was long, though. *So long*. I was so tired. I knew it was the chemo, and I was going to have to get through it somehow. But how? The whole week stretched out ahead of me.

Long, long days of pushing myself through this fatigue every minute of the day. And then the realization that it wasn't just this one week. This was going to go on for months, and every other week, I'd have a really tough Monday like this. How would I ever cope??

The still, small Voice broke into my anxiety and said in my heart, "Trust Me, Jessie. One day at a time. Trust Me." And there it was again. That amazing peace putting my heart and mind at rest. It settled me. It allowed me to let go of the big 'cancer monster' and focus on my patients and my work. When the next patient arrived in the recovery room, I was ready and waiting.

"You're going to love this guy," Chad, the anesthesiologist, told me.

He gave me his verbal report as I quickly and expertly attached the monitoring devices.

"Straightforward left knee replacement. He had the right knee done a couple years ago. He's pretty healthy, but he is a smoker, so watch his oxygenation levels."

Chad reached up and adjusted the oxygen flow level as he spoke. "He's been trying to quit for the past few weeks. Other than that, his vitals have been stable for me, and it was a pretty smooth procedure. Before surgery, he told me he's got a pretty high pain tolerance, so you might not need to give him anything, but I put orders in for morphine and Zofran just in case."

"Ok, thanks. Any output?"

"200cc's. That's his second bag of fluids, so he's had 1700cc's in, 300 up. No allergies to worry about."

Chad signed his paperwork and handed it to me, then turned to the patient.

"Allen? Hey, Allen, how ya feelin'?"

I watched as Allen blinked a few times and struggled to focus. Then he pulled a sleepy crooked half grin and gave a thumbs up to Chad.

"Way to go, Partner. It's all done. You did great! Are you in any pain?"

Allen managed a weak, "Nope, all good."

"Good, that's what we like to hear. I'm gonna leave you here with Jessie. She's gonna take good care of you. I'll stop by a little later to see how you're doing."

He left, and Allen gave me a smile and said, "Good guy."

I smiled warmly. "Yes, he's one of my favorite anesthesiologists. You've been in good hands. So, this is your second rodeo, huh?"

I breathed deeply through a wave of nausea as I charted his vital signs.

"Yeah, I had the other one done almost five years ago. Couldn't stand the pain anymore, so it's time to bite the bullet and get this one done." Allen grimaced as he shifted his position in the bed slightly.

"Are you having some pain now? I can get you something for it."

Allen chuckled. "No, actually, I was expecting it to hurt, so I guess I frowned and gritted my teeth for nothing. Wow, I'm impressed! With the last one, the pain was way outta control already. That guy really knows his stuff! I should've come here for my last surgery, but I was down in Florida then."

"Well, I'm glad it's not hurting but don't wait to tell me if you need something. We want to stay ahead of the pain instead of fighting to get it back under control. Same goes for any nausea."

I walked over to a side table and picked up a jug of ice water I'd prepared ahead of time. A large inflatable cuff was attached to the jug via a tube. I carried it over to a table near Allen's bed.

"This is called a cryo-cuff. I'm going to wrap this cuff around your knee over top of the surgical dressing."

After applying the cuff, which looked much like a huge blood pressure cuff, I attached a bracket to Allen's hospital bed. I then placed the jug of ice water in the bracket, making sure it was securely fastened in.

"This will hold the jug stable for you while you're here. Now when I plug it in and turn it on, this cuff around your knee will fill with ice water, surrounding your knee to provide pain relief and keep the swelling down. When you're discharged home, hopefully tomorrow, they'll teach you how to use it, and you'll take this jug and cuff home with you."

"Well, that's pretty cool," laughed Allen, "pun intended. I wish I'd had this with my first knee replacement."

As Allen continued to become more alert, his jokes and wisecracks kept me laughing so that I hardly noticed the nausea for once.

Hearing the laughter, Chad walked in. "I see you've become the victim of our resident jester," he smiled at me, then at Allen. "Still doing ok, Partner?" He looked over my shoulder to see the trending of Allen's vital signs, then up at the monitor to check his heart rhythm.

"Good, I see Jessie's got your cryo-cuff going. Not in any pain?"

"Man, where were you guys when I got the first knee done? You people are great! No pain, and I'm actually a person to you all instead of just another assembly line job."

Allen smiled warmly at Chad and shook his hand. "Thank you. I really appreciate all you've done."

Chad smiled too. "It's been my pleasure, Allen. But you're not free of me quite yet. I'll be checking in on you tomorrow morning before you leave. I have a meeting I've gotta get to now. Get a good night's rest."

Very soon after, it was time for Allen to be transferred out of recovery and into an in-patient room. I called my patient report to the nurse out on the Med-Surg floor and then called the surgical aide, Madeline, to help me push Allen's hospital bed down the hallway to the correct room. I introduced him to his assigned nurse, amid more jokes and laughter.

"Watch out, Tracy, this guy's a troublemaker," I warned the nurse jokingly. Then I smiled at Allen. "Thank you very much for the entertainment today. I can't tell you how much I needed those laughs."

"Hey, no problem at all. Thank you for taking such good care of me."

Allen shook my hand, and I was smiling as I went back to the recovery room. Allen was my last patient today, and he'd been a great one.

As I cleaned up the recovery room, getting it ready for the next day – or any emergency surgeries that might happen after hours – I thanked God for His constant goodness. He'd helped the last two hours of my work day to sail by easily and with healing humor.

I found that the nausea while working reminded me of how it felt to work while pregnant. Constant waves of it varied in size. Over time I learned to handle it and just be very careful of what I ate.

The weakness and fatigue weren't so manageable. The only variation I noticed in these was that they were both on a steady, gradual increase. And so it went every day for ten days – until the dreaded Thursday rolled around again.

CHAPTER SEVENTEEN

My next infusion was going to be different. The third one. This time they'd leave the awful needle in my chest, and I'd have to take the 'football' home with me. As I finished changing out of my surgical scrubs and into my chemo clothes in the locker room that Thursday, I paused while putting my boots on. Wearily I leaned back to close my eyes and just breathe in the quietness of the moment. Then I resolutely stood up and gathered my things. Time to face the music.

I met Mom in the front lobby.

"Ready?" Mom hugged me and smiled gently.

"Nope. Not even close." I sighed. "Let's do this." I took her arm, and together, we walked to the Infusion Center. Michelle checked us in and put the ID band on my wrist.

"Right this way, ladies," a smiling Bree led us to a curtained-off patient area in the middle of the row of recliners.

She kept up a steady stream of small talk as she got my vital signs and checked my ID band. Then she brought warm blankets for me, and drinks for both of us.

"I remembered to make you some coffee, but it's kinda weak. I thought that might be easier on your stomach. And Mom, here's your Sprite."

After she got us all settled, she left to check on my orders and get the sterile supplies she needed to access my port. I cringed inwardly. I'd already come to hate having my port accessed and flushed. But I said nothing and smiled up at Bree when she returned.

"How's your brother, Bree? Any better?" Bree had told me at my second infusion that her brother was in the hospital in another town. He had a bad case of COVID and was in the ICU unit on a ventilator.

"We've all been praying for him."

I had gotten Bree's permission to share his first name and medical condition with my family and ask them to pray for him.

"He's a little better. Sometimes trying to breathe on his own. But they haven't been able to wean him off the vent yet. Thank you for asking. And for praying!"

Bree went on to tell me a bit more of the medical specifics of her brother's condition as she prepared my skin for the insertion of the sterile needle.

"Ok, now on the count of three, take a deep breath. One, two, three!"

I took a deep breath and felt the needle puncture my skin and enter the port. I did my best to ignore the pain and my emotional reactions. I was slowly getting used to it, but that didn't make me hate it any less.

Bree finished securing the needle in place, then flushed the attached tubing with sterile saline. It flushed easily. Ok, first hurdle over with.

The rest of the infusion went much like the first two had. I played games with Mom, stared out at Lake Michigan, read my book a little, and fell asleep. Once again, I was awakened by the loud beeping of the IV pump. Mom was packing up our things.

Cocooned and comfy in the heated chair and warm blankets, I didn't want to move. I didn't want to face the reality of what came next.

But here was Bree talking gently and quietly about the 'football'. I reluctantly sat up so I could pay attention.

"Ok, Jessie, here we go. The good thing is we don't have to poke you again. And the 'football' is pretty small, just a little larger than a softball." Bree pulled the 'football' out of the protective bag it came from the pharmacy in.

"Oh," I said, "that looks a lot like the infusion balls we used with patients in Home Health care."

"Yup," Bree said. "It works exactly the same. I'll hook it up to the extension tubing you already have attached to the needle in your port. Then it will just do its own thing. You won't have to mess with it at all. It will infuse itself slowly over roughly 36 hours. When you notice the ball is all shrunken and empty except for the hard core, just come in and register at the ED desk. Since it'll always be on a Saturday and the Infusion Center is closed on the weekends, they'll have to page the House Supervisor to either come get you or else meet you here in the Infusion Center. We'll give the House Supervisors a heads-up every time to expect you. They'll disconnect everything, flush the tubing with saline and heparin, then remove the needle and set you free."

I frowned. "It seems like it'd pull and possibly come out when I'm sleeping or changing clothes. What would I do then?"

"I don't plan to let that happen," Bree smiled. "I've hooked these up a few hundred times, so I've come prepared. First, you'll notice that when I accessed your port today, I used a bigger Tegaderm and secured it firmly. That way, it's still a see-through dressing we can keep an eye on, but also safer for longer protection of the site."

She held up a large, wide roll of medical tape. "Also, the tubing is long for that very reason. Once you're all hooked up, I'm going to tape the extra tubing down the middle of your chest all the way to your belly." She held up a small black bag. "This is a sort of fanny pack you'll keep fastened around your waist to carry the 'football' in. That way, a length of tubing will still allow free movement, even in your sleep, while ensuring the needle stays in place."

I held still while Bree hooked up the 'football' tubing to my port tubing. Then with my clothes out of the way, she began taping it down the middle of my chest. It felt strange and a little cold. When Bree was done, I scooted to the front edge of my recliner and put the fanny pack around my waist, adjusting the strap length and clicking the clasp together.

Bree placed the 'football' in the fanny pack along with some gauze pads just in case it leaked at all. "You can wear the fanny pack under your shirt, or loosen the belt strap a little and tuck your shirt under it so you don't have to feel the strap against your skin. Whichever way you're most comfortable. Just be mindful of the little bit of tubing coming up out of the fanny pack."

I tried both ways and discovered I didn't like feeling the belt strap against my skin, so I opted to tuck my shirt under it. I looked down at it and saw that it just looked like I had a normal fanny pack on. Somehow that eased some of my discomfort but not nearly all. I could still very much feel the needle in my chest. The deep sting of it never went away and was distracting.

But as we went home and had exactly the same kind of evening as on the days of the first two infusions, I found I really was able to just relax and take it in stride. I was sure I'd never sleep that night, but I slept great, even with the fanny pack on.

All the next day, the needle and the fanny pack were a constant nuisance, but surprisingly nothing more. I regarded them as exactly what they were – ongoing treatment. Almost like I'd never left the Infusion Center.

And like the day after the other two treatments, I had no energy and no appetite and slept snuggled up in my recliner most of the day.

Saturday morning, I woke suddenly. My very first thought was that this morning I got to get rid of the 'football' and needle. Eagerly I sat up and unzipped the fanny pack. I picked up the 'football' and looked at it. Sure enough, it was shriveled and empty except for the hard core in the middle.

Unfortunately, hurrying was out of the question. Chemo treatments seemed to mess with my head a little, and I always had to move slowly for a few days after one. Pacing myself carefully, I got dressed and slowly went down the stairs. My parents were sitting at the dining room table, finishing up their daily breakfast of coffee with two pieces of toast each. Their toast was always slathered with Mom's homemade jam. Yummy! But not today.

Thankfully the smell was mild, and my nausea didn't flare up too badly.

"Sooooo are we almost ready? It's time to go get this thing out!"

I didn't bother to try for patience. I was more than ready to pass off my 'football'.

Dad put down his coffee cup and chuckled. "Yup, we just got done. I'll be right there."

I went to get my coat and boots on, and Dad soon joined me. He kissed Mom goodbye, and we were off.

Twenty-five minutes later, I was checking in at the ED registration desk. They'd been expecting me and immediately paged the House Supervisor, who happened to be Darren, a nurse I'd worked with often in the ED. Soon, I was walking with him to the Infusion Center.

"So, this was a shock to me," Darren said. "Do you mind if I ask what happened, Jessie? I had no idea you were having trouble."

I couldn't help it. I laughed. "Where do I start? Describing this whole journey would take a while. But the condensed version is that I had a colonoscopy, and they found a cancerous tumor. So here I am on chemo." I shrugged.

"Wow, I'm so sorry! Why do bad things always happen to good people?" Darren shook his head sadly.

But I smiled. "You know, Darren, chemo is awful. I hate it, and I wouldn't wish it on anybody. But the moment I found out about it, my first response was, *God, please just get glory from this*. Ever since then, in every hard situation when I felt I couldn't handle anymore, I've suddenly been filled with a peace so deep, I can't begin to describe it. It's amazing! And honestly, I've gotten to a place where I'm realizing that if it had to happen to anyone in my family, I'd want it to be me. I'm the only one who doesn't currently have anyone directly dependent on me. I have the medical background to mostly understand it all. But I also have this huge support system of friends and coworkers like you all over this hospital, who have helped me in every way they could with such kindness! I'm not alone in this, and I am going to get through it."

Darren gently put his hand on my shoulder.

"You've always been such a wonderful person, Jessie. I'm honored to call you my friend, and I'm proud to be included in those who get to help you through this."

He turned then and unlocked the door to the Infusion Center. "Well, here we are." He gestured to the row of recliners. "Pick a seat and make yourself comfortable. I'll get the supplies so we can turn you loose from that needle."

As I sat in the nearest recliner and turned its heater on, I reflected on what I'd said to Darren.

Did I just witness about God to Darren of all people?! He's not a believer. But it all just flowed right out of my mouth! I didn't even think about it. I wonder what he thinks?

And then I realized it. *Father God, thank You for opening my mouth to glorify You. I want to praise You in all I do. Whatever Darren thinks about it, I want to keep glorifying You. You have my heart and my will.*

Soon, Darren returned with all the necessary supplies and started setting them up on the table. At his request, I told him in more detail what my journey so far had entailed.

"Wow! You've really been through it these past couple months!" Darren shook his head in wonder. "And yet you're still smiling. You're still working. You're still upbeat and positive. I mean, I can see that you're exhausted and don't feel that great, but it sure isn't stopping you!"

He'd finished disconnecting the 'football' by now and flushed the extension tubing to the needle in my port with first saline, followed by heparin.

I grimaced at the now familiar taste of the heparin, as my senses somehow picked it up with the flush.

"Ok, deep breath on three, so I can pull the needle out. One, two, three." I took a deep breath, and Darren quickly and smoothly pulled the needle out of my port. He swabbed the needle entry site on my chest and applied a Band-Aid over the area.

I finally relaxed a bit. Then thoughtfully, I said, "I really can't take the credit for all that. I'm no hero. I actually feel weak most of the time. Sometimes it's just hard, and I wanna quit trying. But then that amazing peace comes, and I hear God saying, 'I'm right here with you. I won't leave you alone. Lean on Me and trust Me,' and it's like my eyes clear, and I can lift up my head and keep going."

Darren was quiet for a moment as he cleaned up the supplies.

"I'm so glad you're in such a good place with this, Jessie. You know as well as I do, how a positive attitude can affect your progress. But I know you. If anyone could remain positive through something like this, it's you. And don't sell yourself short. You're stronger than you think."

He smiled and led me to the door.

"I have to stay and dispose of the 'football' and then do the charting. But you know your way out."

I leaned against the wall for a moment, fighting a wave of nausea.

"Are you ok? You're not feeling too weak or anything? Cuz, I could get you a wheelchair." Darren hovered closer and put his hand on my arm.

"No, I'm ok. It was just the nausea. It's always there, but it comes and goes, in stronger waves sometimes. It's passing now. I'm ok to walk to the car. Thanks, Darren. It's been really good to see you."

Daren spontaneously hugged me. "My pleasure, Jessie. You take care of yourself. I work every other weekend, so hopefully we'll get to do this again."

We smiled at each other, then he stepped back, and I made my way slowly down the hall to the exit.

"Aaaahhhh freedom!" I said as Dad helped me into the car.

"I bet it feels good to get that thing off," Dad smiled. "I can't imagine having to live with that thing attached to you like that."

"Well," I said, "I guess it could be worse."

"Yes. Yes it could. So, how'd it go in there? I hope it wasn't too bad."

I smiled, relieved.

"Nah, I've had worse." Then my tired face lit up. "But I got to witness to someone!" I proceeded to tell Dad the whole story.

"Praise God!" Dad swallowed hard, trying to contain his emotions. "I'm so proud of you, Jessie."

"It was all God, Dad. He gets all the credit. I don't know if anything will ever come of it for Darren, but that's up to God. I'm just happy He gave me His words to speak, and I got the chance to glorify Him in this."

I was smiling as my eyes drooped closed.

Just like the days following the first two infusions, I spent the remainder of the weekend resting a lot. It became a regular thing for Mom and me to sit at the dining room table for a couple hours a day playing our favorite marble and dice board game, Aggravation. It was relaxing for both of us, as it didn't require much thought or energy.

In those hours, the two of us were able to share some of our thoughts and hearts with each other. The bond between us was deepened and strengthened daily. Jetta hung out with us as much as possible, often bringing her husband, Bill, with her to play Wizard, our favorite card game, in the evenings.

That next week I got a surprise visit. Jude came up to visit with his Aunt Sienna, his dad's sister. I was so excited to see them! Sienna and I had always loved each other, and Sienna had gone through breast cancer just over a year ago. And since Jude's two-year stint in Japan, I treasured even more the times I got to spend with him.

For our lunch, Mom made a delicious pot of *chicken a la king* and some biscuits to pour it over.

"I can't believe you're actually able to eat, Jessie," Sienna remarked as we were all enjoying the meal.

I smiled.

"I'm a week out from treatment. This is my off week, and my appetite comes back little by little each time. It takes a bit longer to come back each time, but by a week out, I've been able to eat pretty well."

Sienna shared her cancer journey story as we ate, and I sensed a deeper connection with her. With every personal experience she shared, I heard and understood the emotional responses she didn't say out loud. And the emotional and physical tolls each took. It touched me deeply. Here was another heart that really KNEW.

In the afternoon, I went with Jude and Sienna to a local farmers' market. They were having a fall festival with hayrides, a corn maze, and other fun activities. I wasn't up to any of that, though.

"It's cold out here. Let's wander around inside the store." Jude had seen me shivering and offered me his arm. I gladly took it, and Sienna walked close to my other side.

The enticing aromas of fresh apples and baking donuts greeted us as soon as we opened the door. I was suddenly very thankful this was my off week from chemo, so the constant nausea was at its lowest level.

"Mmmmmm it smells wonderful in here!" Jude chuckled as all three of us closed our eyes and smiled, inhaling deeply. "Yeah, we're not leaving without some fresh cider and donuts."

"You got that right," I agreed. "Warm apple cider donuts are the best! But first, let's look around a little."

The little store was packed with people. Happy people. All were searching out the many Michigan-made treasures, and talking about the wonderful smells in the air. Most of the faces were lit with smiles. Often someone would exclaim over a special find and excitedly share it with people around them.

But what I found really special about the place was the obvious love for God shown in the items for sale. It was a public store, but the autumn and Christmas displays were liberally sprinkled with sayings about God and hope, as well as encouraging and thought-provoking Bible verses.

Sienna and I, both Christians, really enjoyed the chance to shop in such a heartwarming place. But Jude was uncomfortable. For my sake, he patiently endured it, staying close to me to lend his arm for support. Eventually, I settled on a couple of small purchases, and we headed toward the entrance to pick up some cider and donuts.

With so many people packing the small store, the checkout line was long. By the time we left the store, I was really tired.

I shivered over and over again on the walk to my SUV. "Oh, it's so cold out here! All those people being in there made it nice and toasty warm."

"You're tired, aren't you, Mom?" Jude was looking closely at my face. "Are you too tired to drive? I know my way around. I can drive if you want me to."

I loved to drive. Everyone who knew me knew I'd always far rather be the driver than a passenger. Jude, on the other hand, had no love for driving and greatly preferred to let others take the wheel. But now, seeing the tired lines on his mom's face, he was relieved when I handed him the keys without hesitation.

"Thanks, Bud. I'm pretty wiped out."

As soon as I was buckled in, I leaned my head against the window.

"Are you sure you still wanna go up to the overlook, Mom?" Jude started the Jeep. "We can skip it if you're too tired."

"No, I really wanna go up and see it," I said. "The fall colors are at their peak right now. This is my favorite time of year, and I refuse to miss it just for this awful chemo. It won't take long, and it's close to home. I'll be alright."

"Ok, then, here," Jude shrugged out of his jacket. "Use this as a pillow till we get there. Do you want your seat leaned back?"

I thanked him and said no, I was comfortable. Jude was again looking at me closely, but my eyes were getting heavy.

"Let's just drive that way, and we'll see how you feel when we get closer," Sienna suggested. I knew Sienna fully understood this fatigue.

"Sounds great," I said, and then fell quiet as the effort to talk was just too much.

The fifteen-minute drive seemed to take no time at all. I awoke to Jude gently shaking my shoulder.

"We're here, Mom."

I tried hard to hide the fact that my fatigue was so deep.

"Oh, cool, let's go see it." I somehow forced my heavy limbs to obey me and got out of the Jeep. Taking Jude's and Sienna's arms, I crossed the road with them.

The view was tremendously beautiful! We stood on a high point overlooking the huge valley. As far as the eye could see, the valley stretched out, filled with riotous color. Autumn in northern Michigan – *Aaahhhh, what a glorious sight!* All three of us took several pictures and took our time just drinking in the beauty of the place.

But all too soon, I had to end it. "I'm sorry, guys, but I really need to go home and rest."

"No apologies, Jessie," Sienna said, putting an arm around me. "I know. I get it. We're happy just to have gotten to spend this time with you."

Arriving back at my parents' house a few minutes later, Jude and Sienna said their goodbyes. It was late afternoon, and they still had a four-hour trip back downstate to get home. My parents circled everyone for prayer, then hugs all around. Dad saw them out to their car and safely on their way.

Meanwhile, I was completely done in. I gratefully collapsed into my recliner and halfway dragged a blanket onto the chair. I was only vaguely aware of Mom working the lever to lift my legs, then tucking me in snugly with a thick blanket. I fell asleep almost immediately. It had been a wonderful day.

CHAPTER EIGHTEEN

For the next few months my life became a predictable cycle. Every other Thursday it began all over again. Work the first half of the day and have a blood draw sometime during the morning. Then punch out and skip lunch, go to my oncology appointment, followed immediately by my chemo treatment. Including taking the 'football' home till Saturday morning when I returned to the hospital to get rid of it. Sleep most of the weekend, slowly recovering my appetite over the next several days. Work eight-hour days Monday through Friday, rest all weekend, work Monday until Thursday and start it all again.

It was a battle. Actually, several battles in one. Thankfully the blood thinner medication I was taking had been switched to pills, so I no longer had to give myself those painful shots. But I felt cold almost all the time. A weird, different kind of cold. It sort of felt like I was cold on the inside and couldn't get warm. And touching anything cold was very painful. I started using my sleeve to open door handles or turn on a faucet; using a towel to pick up silverware and grasp drawer handles.

I had always loved going barefoot, but that was out of the question now. In fact, I often wore two pairs of socks to work and around the house. I wore long sleeves and sometimes long underwear under my scrubs at work. At home, my dad warmed up my car for me and cleaned off the snow; at work a coworker voluntarily cleaned the snow off my car while I sat in it letting it warm up. Touching anything cold made me jerk my hands back as it felt like there were painful electric shocks being sent through my hands and up my arms.

And it wasn't just the cold. Fatigue was a constant. I woke up tired after sleeping soundly. It didn't matter how much rest I got, it was never enough. The feeling of heaviness in my limbs, and even in my head, never subsided. And the fatigue got worse. It was increasing every two weeks alongside nausea. For the first few days after a chemo treatment, I couldn't eat at all. As my appetite gradually came back each time, I noticed that it came back a little more slowly with each consecutive cycle. The nausea, like the coldness and fatigue, never went completely away.

These physical battles were so hard! Combined like they were, I felt weak and vulnerable all the time. I was in foreign territory, as I'd always been physically strong, ready to work and carry the heavy loads.

How am I supposed to handle this, God? My mind knew the correct answer: I wasn't supposed to carry it, I was supposed to let Him carry it. But oh how extremely hard that was!

I knew several cancer patients who were struggling like I was, and some were far worse off than me. Many had lost all their hair, had had multiple surgeries, sores from radiation, and were in a lot of pain.

But then there were those others. The 'super patients' who seemed to just sail right through it all. They made it look so easy – and seeing that, I became ashamed of my weaknesses. In my head I knew that all cancers are different and each person's body responds to treatments differently. But I saw and felt the differences now. Experiencing them was a whole new ballgame. They were my differences. Owning them was a deeply personal pain I couldn't begin to delve into by myself, let alone with anyone else.

I couldn't face asking myself how those others made it look so effortless. That was beyond me. I had no defense against the shame, the feelings of being less-than. I didn't hate that I needed help at times, and I was extremely grateful for all the support from my family and friends. I'd never take that for granted. Having that support system was a huge gift from God! No way could I do this alone. Maybe those 'super patients' could. Maybe they were just innately stronger than me and would have been no matter what the problem or disease. Maybe. I didn't envy them. I was content being me. I did, however, feel very inadequate. A weakling who couldn't handle sickness.

The ever-changing attacks of emotional and mental anguish became ruthless. Depression, anxiety and fear all fought for a hold on me, and often all three won. It was kind of like the pain of shingles, but in my mind.

I had a shingles outbreak on my side a few years ago. The only way I can think to describe that pain is that it felt like long, sharp talons digging deeply into my body. It was a nagging pain too; like a molar trying to break through a sore, sensitive, swollen gum in the mouth. This 'brain pain' was similar. Sharp, deep, nagging pain in my mind. Depression, anxiety, and fear would each dig their talons in, sometimes individually, sometimes simultaneously.

Now add all that to a body that's dreadfully weak, and continually getting weaker. A body that's constantly nauseated, but needs food it doesn't want, in order to keep functioning. A body that's so fatigued it can barely walk across the floor, and no matter how much rest and sleep it gets, it's not nearly enough.

Combine that tortured mind and that beleaguered body, and try to force them to pull together and get up each morning, get dressed, and somehow get through a full day of work.

Yeah, cancer really does suck.

It sucks the feeling of life out of you. It tries its best to suck away even the will to fight back.

During those long months of chemo treatments, I often felt like I was holding on by my fingernails. By the skin of my teeth. But hold on I did. Or, to be more accurate, I was held on to.

In his book Gentle and Lowly, Dane Ortlund says it like this:

"When my two-year-old Benjamin begins to wade into the gentle slope of the zero-entry swimming pool near our home, he instinctively grabs hold of my hand. He holds on tight as the water gradually gets deeper. But a two-year-old's grip is not very strong. Before long it is not he holding on to me but me holding on to him. Left to his own strength, he will certainly slip out of my hand. But if I have determined that he will not fall out of my grasp, he is secure...So with Christ. We cling to him, to be sure. But our grip is that of a two-year-old amid the stormy waves of life. His sure grasp never falters. Psalm 63:8 expresses the double-sided truth: 'My soul clings to You; Your right hand upholds me.'"

THAT'S my GOD!!!

My favorite saying, my most consistent response to all the turmoil, became, "But God..."

Jetta, our parents and I made that our focus through it all.

And battle after battle was waged.

I feel so, so alone... But God has given me all these people who care so much about me and He promised He'd 'never leave me nor forsake me.

I can't face another chemo treatment and the sick, helpless feeling of neediness afterwards... But God promised He will sustain me and hold me up.

I feel so completely weak… But God is my strength, my ever-present help in trouble.

What if…what if…what if…??? But God will work it all together for my good.

I discovered to my amazement and delight that when I responded to my problems with Scripture, I was enveloped in peace. When I turned my eyes on Jesus, everything that tried to weigh me down was not mine to carry anymore. The more I gave God the glory for all the merciful gifts in my life, the more joy I experienced in the journey. And the more I worshiped Jesus, the deeper my faith became, so that instead of holding on by my fingernails, my hand was being held firmly by the warm, strong hand of my King.

Oh the freedom and wonder of these discoveries!!

Yes, the battles continued. Yes, chemo was still absolutely horrible.

But GOD was there!!!

That was when I began to use my recovery time more wisely. I started by composing letters to Jude, Jamie and Matt. These three I treasured as 'my' children, even though Matt wasn't technically related to my family at all. I knew that the love I bore for each of them was from God. I desperately wanted each of them to know Him and love Him. So far only Jamie did.

In fact, it had partially been Jamie's faith and witness for Jesus that had led me back to Him. So now, in trying to prepare for the biggest 'what if?', I wrote out my testimony to each of them. Each letter was very personal and very focused on my love for Jesus. and how that love was the fountain from which came the depth of my affection for each of them. When I was finished writing the letters, I had my mom put them in the fireproof safe box along with my will.

Next, I began to order my finances. I drafted a list of the specifics, including checking and savings account numbers, credit card account numbers, and all expenses I was responsible for each month. This list too I had my mom put in with my will.

Finally, I began to plan my funeral. I'd always seen this as kind of a morbid exercise, but now I found it wasn't that way at all. Digging through my Bible for favorite verses to be shared, turning the pages of an old beloved hymnal and rediscovering songs I used to love and hadn't heard in a long time. It was a fun process of revisiting the ways God had shown me His love through all the years of my life. I was humbled, amazed and oh so thankful!

CHAPTER NINETEEN

But when the COVID pandemic caused the hospital's increasing precautions to include prohibiting someone to come with me to chemo treatments, I wanted to give up. No way could I go in there alone! It was way too heavy; way too much to demand of any chemo patient. Bitter thoughts assailed me.

Obviously, they've never gone through anything like this themselves. They have no idea what this is like. How can they seriously expect anyone to face this alone?!

The darkness threatened to completely engulf me and I felt weaker and more vulnerable than ever.

BUT GOD was my light! Suddenly all those Scriptures I'd been using as weapons began shining through the darkness. And the darkness could not withstand that Light. Never had I KNOWN the Presence of God like I did that day. I walked into the Infusion Center filled with the peace of His Presence. I smiled warmly at Bree and the other staff, and they looked surprised.

"Wow, I'm relieved to see you smiling, Jessie." Then Bree lowered her voice so only I could hear. "Everyone today has been so upset and anxious about having to come here alone. It's been a really hard day for all of us." Bree's voice was sad. Then she smiled. "So, what's your secret? New boyfriend or something?"

I laughed. A carefree, happy sound that turned several heads our way.

"Nope. I'm just really thankful. I mean look around! We're in a warm, beautiful place with an amazing view out these huge windows. We have wonderfully skilled people like you taking great care of us. It's a gorgeous, sunshiny day outside." I shrugged.

"So maybe my family isn't here to play games with me and take my mind off the chemo. That's ok. I know they're praying for all of us. And I've got my Bible here. That's enough any day!"

As my infusion began and I settled into my warm recliner, I talked quietly with Bree about how afraid I'd been to come alone and the peace God had given me. Bree was quiet for a few moments, then said, "I could really use some of that peace."

"What's wrong? Is it your brother? Is he any better?" Bree was almost never negative, so I was immediately concerned. As far as I knew, Bree's brother was still on a ventilator due to COVID. Now I worried that he'd taken a bad turn.

"Actually, he's a lot better! He's awake and hoping to be discharged home soon."

My mouth dropped open. "Wow, that's wonderful! We've really been praying for him. I can't wait to tell Jetta!"

Bree gave me a huge smile. "I knew you'd pray. Thank you so much! I think it saved him."

"Then what's the problem?"

"Well, you saw how down everyone was when you got here. This 'no visitors' rule is a huge deal for chemo patients. You know how hard it is to come in here WITH a visitor. But now... well people are pretty emotional about it. Some are angry and vocal, some are crying, some are so anxious they're nauseated before they even start treatment. It's been a pretty rough week."

"Oh, I'm so sorry! And I'm ashamed I was only seeing it from the patient point of view. I should have realized this would be really hard on all of you too! I wish there was something we could do to help people."

At that moment my cell phone buzzed. "It's a text from Jetta. I think we're going to get our wish!"

"How?"

"Jetta says look out the window, down on the lawn outside."

Bree and I went to the huge curved window in front of the row of chemo recliners and looked down. There, on the lawn beside the hospital, were Jetta, her two kids, Ian, and our mom all holding huge signs. The signs were for me and for all the cancer patients.

YOU ARE NOT ALONE!

WE ARE PRAYING FOR YOU!

CHEMO WARRIORS, GOD CARES AND WE CARE!

JESSIE WE LOVE YOU!

I stood there covering my mouth, tears streaming down my face. I looked at Bree and saw the tears shimmering in her eyes too. Then we both began to call out to all the rest of the chemo patients there.

"Come up close to the window! Look down on the lawn!"

The effect was amazing. Several were crying or near tears. All were smiling and waving. Suddenly everyone felt like a team; like they were in this together, not alone. A few minutes was all it took. As Jetta and company packed up the signs and got in her van to leave, the whole mood of the place was changed. It was like Hope had made an appearance and left a deep impression on each person – patient and staff alike.

From that time on, Jetta made it a bi-weekly mission to gather a group of people to make more signs and go to the hospital to hold them up for the chemo patients during my treatments. Every other week when I arrived at the Infusion Center the other patients would ask if the signs were coming that day. They all looked forward to it, wondering aloud what the signs would say this time.

Then one Thursday my sister Jada came up to visit. The ban on visitors was still partially in effect, but she was able to accompany me to my treatment! She had previously been there once to join Jetta in making and holding up signs outside the window. This time Jada, also a nurse, walked into the Infusion Center at my side. I introduced her, my oldest sister, to all the staff. Jada was sweet and kind. Without thinking about it, she automatically performed the nursing tasks of assisting me into my recliner, raising my feet, turning on the recliner's heater, and tucking warm blankets in around me.

"Once a nurse, always a nurse, huh?" I laughed. "Better be careful Sis, cuz everyone around here is short-staffed thanks to COVID. They might try to keep you and put you to work."

Jada laughed too.

"I would apologize, but my heart's not in it."

Then more quietly she said, "But honestly, Jessie, this is one of those times I'm so thankful God made me a nurse. I'm honored to have the privilege of helping to take care of my beloved 'Little' sister."

We looked at each other. Both of us had tears in our eyes. Both understood on a level few others could. Giving nursing care was second nature to us after all these years. But this was special. It felt as if we each had been brought through all those years of nursing experience caring for others in order for us to share the intimate connection of this very moment.

"I confess, sometimes it's really hard to be the patient instead of the nurse," I said. "I'm a care-Giver, not a care-Receiver. But today I'm so thankful. God amazes me!"

Bree came then and began preparing to access my port. This was an old routine to me by now, but Jada was impressed.

"You came prepared," she said. "When we were getting all bundled up to leave the house, I wondered why you'd worn such an open-necked shirt during the winter. Now I get it. It makes the port easy to get to."

"Yeah," I said, "Before I started chemo my friend Dana told me what to wear. This is now my 'chemo shirt'. I wear it to all my infusions." Then, after pausing a moment, I said, "But I think I'm gonna burn it when I'm done with chemo!"

With my permission, Jada chatted with Bree about the specifics of my medications, lab results, and chemo treatments. Her nurse mind needed to understand this on a medical level.

"You make that look easy!" Jada marveled at my calmness as Bree expertly pushed the needle through the skin of my chest and into my port. "Anyone would think you two have done this a few times."

Bree and I both laughed. "Make that a few thousand times on my end," Bree said. "But you're right. It must be awful, but Jessie always does it without any local anesthetic or freeze spray. She's a real trooper."

I shrugged noncommittally. "Eh, it's just a poke. Needles have never really bothered me. I used to let fellow nursing students, and later paramedic students, practice starting IVs on me. No biggie. But boy you should've seen me the first time we went through this! I sure wasn't calm about it that day. At least not on the inside."

Bree brought me some hot, black coffee without having to ask. She knew by now what I liked. "And for you?" she asked Jada.

Before Jada could answer, I blurted out, "Coke. No contest."

"What can I say," laughed Jada. "It's the best!"

"I miss cold drinks," I said as Bree left to get Jada's Coke. "I hope someday I can have a chocolate shake again."

"What happens if you drink something cold?"

I shuddered, remembering the day I'd tried to take my pills with water that was slightly cool instead of warm. "It's horrible! My throat immediately spasms; it sort of seizes and closes up. It feels kinda like you're choking, but worse. It's not exactly painful, just awful and scary."

"Wow! Yikes! I know it hurts if you touch something cold, but to not be able to drink anything cold... I can't imagine." Jada shook her head, looking at me. "I'm really sorry you have to go through all this, Jessie."

I resolutely held up my coffee cup. "Well, at least I can still usually handle coffee." I smiled. "Ya gotta find the silver lining." Then I dropped my eyes and quietly admitted, "To tell you the truth, I hate getting my port accessed. I REALLY hate it. It's not the discomfort. That's so minor. I think it's the connotations with the chemo and how sick and weak it makes me feel. Anyway, I really have to prepare myself for it. The smells, the feel, all of it."

The two of us were quiet for a moment, then I felt the need for smiles. "Let's play a game. What do we have?"

We played a card game, then the family favorite with the Scrabble tiles. After a while I made my slow way to and from the bathroom, again, pulling my IV pole along with me and using it to steady myself. As soon as I returned, Jada helped me get cozied up to sleep.

When the infusion was finished, Jada watched with interest as Bree hooked up the 'football' for me to take home until Saturday. Bree explained it all to her as I quietly submitted to the process.

Afterward Jada helped a sleepy and slightly unsteady Jessie to get my boots, coat, hat, scarf, and mittens on. Thanking Bree, she assisted me out to Jetta's waiting van. I was so weak and tired, I fell asleep again as soon as we arrived home and I'd made it to my recliner.

CHAPTER TWENTY

Infusion, sleep, work, sleep... infusion, sleep, work, sleep... On and on it went.

At every oncology appointment, immediately before I left for my chemo infusion, the oncologist or his Nurse Practitioner would ask if I was having any numbness or tingling in my hands or feet. I hadn't experienced any symptoms like those and always wondered at those questions. Numbness and tingling didn't seem to go with nausea, weakness, and fatigue at all unless one was dehydrated. So I always explained my extreme weakness and fatigue, and that these were accompanied by constant underlying nausea. But no, no numbness or tingling.

I was trying hard to tough it out. I felt I needed to work as much as possible. It was my responsibility to pull my weight. Besides, I loved my job and the people I worked with. I thought that if I could just force myself through, I'd reach a point where the symptoms were stabilized.

But my body wasn't buying it. Treatment piled on top of treatment and I was taking longer and longer to recover enough to sort of function normally. And my appetite was now taking at least a week to begin to return. About two-thirds of the way through my treatments, the weakness and fatigue became such a huge burden that I had to approach my manager again.

"I'm sorry," I said, hanging my head. I was once more standing in my manager's office. Once more overcome with shame at my limitations. "You said to tell you if it was getting to be too much for me. I know I'm already below forty hours, but I can't recover fast enough anymore. I need to start taking off the Mondays right after an infusion. I'm so weak and exhausted!"

"Oh, Jessie, I'm glad you told me! Of course you can do that. Honestly, I'm shocked you've been able to work so much for so long."

I still felt awful. "I'm so sorry I'm leaving you all short-handed. I've been fighting having to do this, but I just physically can't do it anymore."

"Please don't worry about us," my manager smiled. "You're a trooper. A hard worker. You've hung in there through all these months, and through some really tough days. I'm proud of you. Don't worry about the staffing. That's my job. We'll be fine. You just take care of you. I'll make the schedule changes right now."

"Thank you for understanding and helping me through all this," I said. Then I quickly excused myself.

That extra day of rest and recovery after my infusions helped immensely. It wasn't a total fix, and I still had to fight hard to get myself through the work days. But at least I was able to get to a slightly better place physically before facing it.

I had just begun to think I was going to make it. I'd finished almost all of my infusions. Only two more to go. I was going to be a huge success story. I was going to be one of the rare patients who was able to keep working all the way through chemo and beyond. The end was in sight.

Of course, that's when it all falls apart, right?

The day before my second to last chemo treatment, I awoke in the morning feeling strange. At first, I couldn't figure out what was different. But as I sat up on the side of the bed, I swayed and almost fell sideways. The room felt unstable; almost shaky. I decided to stand up slowly and see if that weird feeling went away.

But where were my feet? I knew I'd sat up on the edge of the bed, so my feet should be on the floor. I looked down. Sure enough, both of my feet were flat on the floor. I moved them against the carpet, and that's when I began to be afraid. I was watching my own feet moving against the floor, but I couldn't feel anything at all. It was like they weren't attached to me; like they were somebody else's feet pretending to be mine. They may as well have been a couple of blocks of wood sitting there at the end of my legs.

I lifted my hand in front of my face and looked at it. I opened and closed it a few times. I watched as my thumb obeyed my thought to rub against a fingertip – but there was no sensation of touch!

Suddenly frightened, I began touching my skin all over my body... *Nothing!* Complete numbness all over. Looking down again, I lifted one foot and brushed it down the opposite shin.

And almost screamed. Painful shocks were running through my arms and legs. They came in waves. Unpredictable. They didn't seem to be associated with any certain movement, nor with stillness. And they hurt!

The thought entered my mind, *THIS is what they call numbness and tingling?!*

What an understatement!

Slowly, I tried to stand up. I desperately needed to pee, and the bathroom was only a short distance across the upstairs landing of my parents' home. However, my head no longer seemed to be connected to the rest of my body and I fell back on the bed.

"Ok, Jessie, you can do this. You HAVE to do it. Slowly now. Hold onto the furniture and walls. Take your time..."

My bladder was screaming for a much faster trip across the little landing, but I had no choice. Slowly, so slowly, clutching whatever furniture was in reach, pressing my numb body against the wall for support, I made it to the bathroom – where I made yet another awful discovery.

It was easy as ever to pee in the toilet normally, but that's where 'normal' ended. I had to watch my numb hands pull and tear off some toilet paper. So far so good... But my WHOLE body was numb. Not only could I not feel the toilet paper in my hand, I couldn't feel the toilet paper wiping my body.

This is NOT ok! I'm numb all over! And ouch, these shocks in my arms and legs hurt! How am I supposed to walk when I can't feel my feet? Oh no! How in the world am I going to get down all those stairs? And work! No way can I go to work like this! I'm gonna hafta call in sick. I can't even drive right now. And what's with my head? How come I feel like I'm gonna fall over all the time?

Holding onto the sink for dear life, I forced all of my concentration into brushing my teeth. Then I slowly and carefully made my way back across the landing to my bedroom. Scared and needing comfort, I pulled on some warm sweats and a loose, but warm sweatshirt. Thick wool socks were a must, but between the weakness, the numbness, and the sharp shooting pains I couldn't get them on! So I put the socks in my pocket and shakily made my way to the top of the narrow staircase.

Fifteen steep stairs. My brain rebelled in waves of dizziness at the sight, and the nausea threatened to floor me. Gritting my teeth, I turned sideways. Focusing my attention on both hands gripping the railing, I then made myself look down at my feet. One foot at a time, I concentrated on lifting one leg and then the other, placing one foot and then the other on to the first step down. Then the second. Breathe... Ok, now the third step. Now the fourth.

By the time I reached the foot of the stairs I was mentally exhausted and physically trembling. My dad came around the corner from the dining room into the living room and saw how I was dressed.

"Those don't look like work clothes," he chuckled. Then he saw my face. "Jessie, you're white as a sheet! What's wrong? Are you ok?"

My mom, hearing my dad's questions and concern, hurried into the living room. "Jessie! Are you ok, Baby? What's wrong?"

All of a sudden I was extremely thankful God had guided me to move in with my parents for this journey.

"I'm not doing so great this morning," I said. "You know how they always ask if I have any numbness or tingling? And I always say no? Well, I think I just found out what they were talking about."

Holding onto furniture, I started to make my way across the living room. Dad hurried over and helped and then I sank carefully into my recliner. "I'm numb all over the outside of my entire body. I can't feel anything touching me or that I touch."

"Well, I bet that's a bit challenging," my dad said. "But you don't look like that's all that's going on."

"Yeah, I'm having some pretty bad balance problems. And if this is what they meant by 'tingling', then I've got news for them. It's like electric shocks shooting through my arms and legs just randomly, but really often."

"Oh, Baby! That sounds miserable! You can't go to work this way." My mom hit the nail on the head.

"No, I need to call in," I said. "I just wanted to get down the stairs and explain to you both first."

"You go ahead and call them," Dad said. "Stay right there. I'll get your coffee."

Mom helped tuck my favorite big, thick blanket around me. Then she hovered a bit as I made the call to work. She was obviously and understandably worried. I was too, and trying not to show it.

"I'm going to call the oncology office too," I told my parents as soon as I got off the phone. "But I need to wait until after eight o'clock when it opens. They wanted me to call if anything changed."

Dad had come back carrying my favorite mug full of steaming coffee. "Sounds like a good plan. You sure want them to know. You think they may need to change your medicine or something?"

"Ah, Dad, I just don't know. I'm guessing they'll adjust my chemo doses, but that's just a guess."

After a little more concerned conversation, I leaned back to rest and was soon asleep. I awoke a couple hours later to a sense of deja vu. I could hear my parents talking quietly with Jetta in the next room. Sitting up slowly, I worked the lever to lower my feet to the floor. Immediately, all three of them came into the living room and sat down.

"Ok," I said, "what's the big discussion about this time?"

Jetta and our parents all looked at each other. Then Mom leaned forward. "Jessie, honey, we think it's time for a change. In your present condition it's not really safe for you to be using the stairs anymore."

"So, we're going to switch your room with Mom and Dad's," Jetta explained. "We just didn't want to get started without you knowing."

Tears immediately filled my eyes. I nodded silently, unable to speak. They all understood. Nobody knew what to say. All of us felt a heavy sadness. They knew this was really hard for me. It was scary. Unknown territory. Nobody knew what to expect from it all. The sudden crippling physical problems and the loss of my private little retreat upstairs combined into a monstrous *double whammy*. It almost felt like giving up, similar to acknowledging I might die. Each of us felt it. None of us could make it better.

"Well, let's get started," Dad said and stood up. Coming over to me, he quietly squeezed my shoulder a moment. Then they all got to work. Mom went into their main-level bedroom and started emptying their dresser.

Dad and Jetta headed upstairs to start packing up my things.

And I sat there. I sat there feeling horrible. Two sudden and deeply depressing changes all wrapped up together, and there was literally nothing I could do. I knew better than to even offer to help. Weak and off balance even just sitting still, I couldn't help but feel useless. I couldn't face calling the oncologist just yet. Closing my eyes, leaning my head back, fighting tears, I began to pray.

By lunch time the move was done and the call had been made. Jetta sat with me, holding my cold hands in her warm ones. Both of us were fighting tears.

"I'm so sorry, Jessie. I know this feels hopeless. I so wish this didn't have to happen to you! We don't understand, but we love you so very much!"

"Thank you for all your help, Jetta. I'm so thankful God has surrounded me with such a loving, caring family through all this."

We hugged each other, tears streaming down both our faces. Finally, Jetta pulled slowly away. She had to leave for an appointment. She promised to come back later that afternoon.

From then on, the time when the horrible symptoms caused such huge and immediate changes that terrified us all came to be known as THAT DAY. It gradually became a point of comparison, as in, "Yeah, but it's not nearly as bad as THAT DAY..." It also became a sort of dividing line, as in, "...but before THAT DAY happened, it all seemed kind of predictable."

Better and worse, before and after... In so many ways life had changed dramatically, not just for me, but for Jetta and my parents as well. They lived through it all with me, day after day, surprise after surprise.

None of us knew how long my new, crazy, scary symptoms would last. Over the next couple weeks, we discussed it over and over again. The oncologist had merely tried to commiserate and said each person is different, so we had no real end point to hold on to or look forward to. There was no telling how long it would be. They'd adjusted my chemo dosing, greatly reducing the drug they knew to be the problem. This was in hopes of helping me finish out my prescribed course without making any of my symptoms worse.

After talking again with my manager, I was put on a short-term disability leave until further notice. *Ugh. It's officially true now. I'm officially useless. I can't be a nurse at all now! I wonder if I'll ever work as a nurse again...*

Never had I thought I'd have to use any kind of disability; It hadn't even crossed my mind. Now I was facing a possible complete end to my whole nursing career!

FEAR... Stark and strong it coursed through me. It sickened me to no end. It sapped my waning energy and left me screaming on the inside. Again, I was striving for outward calm while a hurricane raged in my mind and emotions.

I can't do this anymore. I'm not strong enough. This wasn't part of the deal! Please, please, please… I don't even know how to pray or what to pray for. I can't stand this! I'm useless! I've literally become nothing but a burden.

It degenerated fast, until it was a genuine pity party. I cried a LOT during those days. I was a real mess, and part of me knew all the attempts at subterfuge were pointless; my family knew I was a mess inside. Of course, that only made the pity party worse…

CHAPTER TWENTY-ONE

But two weeks later the light at the end of the chemo tunnel shone bright and strong. After almost seven long months, my chemo treatments were finally coming to an end. On the day of my last infusion, I walked into the Infusion Center smiling. My brother Les was with me.

"This is it, girl!" Bree greeted me with a big hug. "How are you feeling?"

I couldn't help but smile through the sick feeling that facing chemo always caused. "Well, I'd say I'll feel better after it's done, but we both know that's a lie," I laughed. "Let's just say I sure won't miss having to face this over and over again. But I'm really gonna miss all of you!"

"I know. We were all just talking about that. We're really gonna miss your smiling face around here. And your family holding up signs outside!"

I hadn't thought about that part. But I thought now that knowing Jetta, she'd continue that for a while because she knew people really looked forward to it.

This was the one chemo treatment my younger brother Les had been able to accompany me to. Les was a pastor and very friendly and outgoing. He joked and laughed with various staff members, bringing smiles to almost everyone there. Having volunteered as a licensed EMT for many years, he understood most of the medical processes involved in giving the chemo infusions, and he was comfortable in hospital situations.

As soon as my infusion was going, Les and I pulled out the Scrabble tiles and began to play. After a while we stopped and just enjoyed the view of Lake Michigan through the huge windows while we talked quietly. Surprisingly, I felt no need for sleep this time. We played cards while we enjoyed the view. I was very pleasantly surprised when Bree came to disconnect me from the main infusion, and hook up the 'football'. The time had gone so fast! How had I stayed awake through the whole thing?

Unknown to me, Les had notified Jetta about the timing of when my treatment would finish. Jetta had picked up our parents, along with Dana, and brought everyone to the hospital. Bree had contacted the surgical department to see if any of them could come to the Infusion Center. Only one nurse coworker could, but he happily showed up.

Finishing chemo treatments is a BIG deal! Every patient who finishes gets to ring the large ship's bell and read a quote at their final exit time.

Bree hooked up the 'football', then Les helped me get my winter stuff on. As we started to walk toward the exit, Jetta came in the side door with Dana and our parents.

"Surprise!" they all called out.

Tears sprang to my eyes. "I so wished you could all be here, but I had no idea you were all really coming!"

I hugged each one, then they escorted me to the bell hanging by the nurses' station. Dana and I stared into each other's teary eyes, sharing a profoundly deep understanding of all that this moment meant. Then Bree handed me a card with a moving quote for me to read aloud so all could hear. When I finished reading – forcing the words out past the tears in my heart – Bree directed me to ring the bell.

I took a moment and looked around. I met the eyes of each person present, silently giving praise to God for this team He had surrounded me with. This family of love. Then I raised my hand and grasped the rope. Looking around at each person once more, I rang that bell loud and happily! Everyone cheered and called out congratulations to me. Almost everyone shed some tears. As I tightly hugged each person, I thanked God for them silently as I thanked them out loud. It was a wonderful celebration!

Now, though, I began to face bigger, deeper mental and emotional battles than ever. Not being able to work – actually being on disability – robbed me of the only definition of *ME* I'd ever known. I was a nurse and I had been a nurse my whole adult life. It was my identity; not just what I did for a living, but *who I was*. So, what was I supposed to do with the leftovers of 'me'? That's what it felt like.

All the way through chemo, I had assumed my symptoms would all resolve quickly after the infusions finished, and I'd progressively regain my strength and soon be able to return to work. Life would pretty much go back to normal and maybe that would have happened if the 'numbness and tingling' hadn't started. That changed everything. Literally every aspect of my life.

The family sat around my parents' kitchen table, talking it over. Bill and Jetta, both our parents, and me. It was hard. I felt completely lost. I was out of my element. As a nurse, I was used to my family looking to me for medical answers, but this time I had none. I had no experience to fall back on. I was facing limitations I'd never even known existed.

"The oncologist doesn't seem to know how long it'll last," I said in answer to my dad's question.

"But they must have some idea," Jetta said. "Other people must have had these symptoms before."

"Well, he says each person is different. Each person's body reacts in its own way."

"What do you think, Jessie? How do you feel?" Mom looked worriedly at her youngest daughter.

I shrugged. "No different yet. Nothing has changed."

"That's disappointing," Dad said. "I would think your symptoms should have started fading almost as soon as they stopped giving you the chemo."

"I hoped they would too. That's how symptoms usually work. But this? I have no idea." I hesitated. "I'm thinking maybe a month? Anyway, that's my best guess right now."

"Well," Dad said, "at least you'll be able to get disability while you heal up. Isn't it amazing how God has provided? He's made sure you'll keep receiving a paycheck while you're unable to work."

"And you can stay here as long as you need to," Mom said. "We'll all help you."

That was that. I stayed with my parents and spent my days resting, reading, playing table games with my mom and sometimes Jetta. Slowly, very slowly, I began to regain a little strength. Day by day, my appetite returned. Little by little, I began to be able to swallow cold drinks and touch cold things again.

But the other symptoms didn't show any sign of fading. In fact, I now noticed I was having more trouble concentrating on things. Even on my favorite things. I'd always loved playing games, but these days I could only play for about an hour before I'd have to stop and rest my mind. I loved to read novels, but lately I had to stop after just two or three chapters. I loved to go for walks, but poor balance and constant fatigue challenged me big time.

Church services, which had finally become a delight to me over the past three years, now required constant struggling to pay attention until the end. Not only that, but my memory was horrible. Things that had happened quite some time ago I was okay with, but things that were recent often fell into what I called holes. My short-term memory became a maze of Swiss cheese. And I had no clue which things would stick and which would fall into a hole. It was all so draining!

Unfortunately, concentration, memory, and balance weren't my only problems. The numbness all over my body persisted. So did the painful 'zingers' of what felt like electric sparks along my nerves, especially in all of my limbs. The pain was horrible and combined with the weird numbness, it made everyday life a series of hard challenges. I began using a wheeled walker to help with balance. I named the walker 'Charlie' and he went everywhere with me.

CHAPTER TWENTY-TWO

My oncologist soon prescribed physical and occupational therapy, PT and OT. The first appointment was called the 'intake assessment'. It focused on figuring out exactly what my diagnoses and limitations were, but it wasn't easy.

"Now we're going to test your distal sensation," Jim, the Physical Therapist, said. I was lying on my back on a cot, barefoot and had my loose pant legs pulled up to my knees. "First, I'm going to use a dull object, and then a sharp object, to touch various areas on your lower legs and feet. You tell me when you feel something and where. Also tell me if you think it's dull or sharp. Ready? Here we go."

I had to concentrate very hard to feel anything at all. Occasionally I felt the tiniest pin prick. Sometimes I felt what might have been a slight pressure. Often, I felt nothing.

That exercise was followed by several others. I was asked to lift one leg at a time, resist various pressures, pick up one foot and rub it down the opposite shin, etc.

Then I put my shoes and socks on and began again. I now had to go from sitting to standing, standing still with feet apart, with feet together, trying to stand on one foot, etc.

"Ok, next I want you to just stand still, with your feet shoulder-width apart, and close your eyes."

"NO!!" I was filled with sudden fear. Almost panic! "I have trouble balancing with my eyes open! I have zero balance when I shut my eyes! I'll definitely fall."

Jim was a little surprised, but then immediately reassured me. "I'll put one hand on your upper chest and one hand on your back. I promise I won't let you fall."

Still afraid, I nevertheless steeled myself to try. Taking a deep breath, then pushing it out slowly, I nodded. "OK, I'm ready."

As I closed my eyes, Jim began counting seconds. "One, two." But my body was already weaving dangerously, swaying like a tree in a windstorm, and my eyes flew open.

"Ok," Jim said. "Ok, you're right. You're not at all ready for that. But that's okay. Sit down and rest."

I sank gratefully into my chair, feeling shaky and still off balance. "That helps me know better what you need as far as physical therapy. With all the testing we've done so far you obviously have true neuropathy. Don't worry. It'll take time and work, but we can help you."

I asked the question I most wanted answered. "How long will I be like this?"

"Well, that's hard to say," Jim hedged. "For some people it resolves fairly quickly. You have a pretty pronounced case of it, though. I think it's safe to say that it's going to take a while."

My heart sank along with my hopes. How long would I have to live this way? And what would happen with my job?

After a brief rest I was sent to the Occupational Therapy intake assessment. There the Therapist, Carrie, put me through more interesting testing. Among other things, Carrie measured the grip strength in each of my hands, assessed my hand-eye coordination, and extensively tested the feeling in my arms and hands. I felt like I flunked it all, but Carrie assured me there was no such thing. She explained that this testing was in order to find my baseline functioning so they could figure out where and how they needed to start treatment for me.

All in all, the initial testing took around two hours. It was decided I would need two sessions of both PT and OT per week, so they scheduled me for a second two-hour session later in the week. The therapists were wonderful, and skillfully guided me through progressive levels. However, the biweekly sessions were demanding, difficult, and painful. My dad drove me to and from each therapy appointment because they completely exhausted me, mentally and physically.

The therapies seemed to last forever, but by the end of those appointments I had discarded the walker. I became comfortable using ski poles to assist my balance, even though grasping them hurt my hands.

When my initial order for PT and OT expired, it wasn't renewed. Instead, since my symptoms were still going strong after a couple of months, my oncologist referred me to a specialist who was an expert in treating post-chemotherapy neuropathy and other symptoms.

During my first appointment with him, he was a bit alarmed at the extent of my physical problems. He did another thorough physical assessment of my strength, balance, coordination, and pain. He prescribed a change in my nerve pain medication as my current prescription didn't seem to be helping. Through screening questions, I also admitted to struggling with many of the symptoms of major depression and anxiety.

"I believe you also need to start on an antidepressant medication," he told me. "However, I'd like to wait just a little while. I think we need a firmer grasp on just how extensive the problems are. I want to refer you to a brain and nerve specialist. He's a neuropsychologist. I want to be sure exactly what we're dealing with, before we take the chance of masking it with an antidepressant."

The specialist ended the appointment by advising me to file immediately for federal aid via social security disability benefits. Especially since my short-term disability through work had now had to switch over to long-term disability. He explained that it would take at least six months, and often a year or more, to get approved and by that time I may be in real need of that assistance.

CHAPTER TWENTY-THREE

So, I found myself facing yet another new doctor. Yet another specialist. Yet another draining assessment process. It was tiring and overwhelming for me to even think about.

"I'm going with you," Jetta insisted. "For one thing, his office is an hour away and you'll be tired. For another, I have psychology training. I'm the perfect second set of ears for this appointment." Jetta had gotten her master's degree and worked as a school psychologist until her kids were born. I was relieved to hear she'd be accompanying me to this appointment.

I had been instructed to expect a one-hour assessment and discussion period with the doctor, then a one-hour break for lunch, then four hours of testing in the afternoon. Jetta was allowed to accompany me for the assessment and discussion period, but would have to wait out in the lobby during the afternoon of testing.

Upon meeting the doctor and discussing my history and present condition, both Jetta and I were pleasantly impressed. He led us through a thorough description of personal life history while he took extensive notes. Together we explained as much as possible, including my family/social status, medical history, psychological status, physical limitations awareness, and future plans. By the end of an hour, he had developed a pretty accurate picture of who I was and what I was facing.

"As with many chemotherapy patients," he said, "you present to me as someone who's been poisoned. That's to be expected with chemotherapy. It's obvious with the extensive neuropathy and loss of sensation that you've experienced damage to the peripheral nervous system. As you know, the peripheral nervous system has the potential to heal itself – very slowly. What we need to figure out then, is whether your central nervous system has also been poisoned. That would be more permanent damage."

I fidgeted. *Poisoned?! I never thought of it that way. Possibly permanent?? No, no no! Oh, Father, I can't do this alone! Help me, please!*

Jetta and I left for our lunch break talking about our impressions of the morning meeting.

"That's a really scary word. Poisoned."

Hearing the fear in my voice brought tears to Jetta's eyes. "But you're still here, Baby, and we're all here with you. It may be a longer road than any of us could have imagined. That's ok. Cuz our Road-Builder is right here with us. He wouldn't have led us here without good reason and He's not about to just leave us here alone."

I lifted my eyes and looked out at the gray, winter waves. Jetta had driven us to Subway to get lunch and we'd decided to eat by the water. I thought of all the suddenness and fear at the beginning of this journey. I remembered every weird, confusing, overwhelming new development. Every diagnosis, every surgery, every treatment, every therapy, every blood draw and infusion. In my mind's eye I pictured each doctor, nurse, therapist, and surgical team I'd received such good care from along the way. There were so many changes, big and small, that myself and my family had to adjust to. So many scary unknowns to face.

It had been less than a year. Only nine months, really. Nine very long, trying months. Nine months of emotional and physical upheaval that at times had brought me to the brink of wanting to give up. Of constant battles, internal and external. Of extreme changes I could never have imagined – and would never have wanted to. Nine months of being forced to need care. Of learning to receive the gifts of loving attention from those I loved most.

Now I fully understood why I'd so often heard dealing with cancer is called a 'Journey'. It truly is. A long, scary, convoluted road with no predictable end.

But like a thick golden strand standing out amongst a million lesser, thinner colors, there for me had been indescribable Peace. It was woven so intricately, so persistently... so SOFTLY through the otherwise rough fabric of this unwanted journey. God had been there every step of the way. He'd not only been there walking beside me; He'd literally carried me many times. In all this reflection, I suddenly realized, I now understood the poem about Footsteps in the Sand on a profoundly deep and personal level. It had always been a favorite. Now, I sensed it becoming my private legacy.

I finally turned to Jetta and said the one thing I could say. The one sentence that seemed ingrained into my very being. "I just want God to get glory from this."

We talked quietly through the rest of the lunch break, then headed back to the office where my testing would take place. As a former psychologist, Jetta had given me some idea of what tests would likely take place.

The afternoon was brutal! Most people going through such testing may not have agreed, but I was already so depleted, mentally and physically. Even though this was all mental testing. A long, exhaustive IQ test, followed by more of the same type of brain-draining questions and activities.

Ugh! Pretty sure I'm flunking everything here. I used to be smart. I prided myself on my intelligence. Guess that's over and done.

At just over two hours, the doctor called it quits for the day. "You're obviously extremely fatigued. Attempting further testing today would be a waste of time for both of us. You're just not up to it. I'd like to stop here for today and schedule you for a second appointment in about two weeks to finish up the second half of the testing. That way you have a good recovery period."

He got no argument from me! I texted Jetta to come pick me up, then went to the desk to make the follow-up appointment. I had to fight sleep sitting in the waiting room chair until Jetta got there. When she did, she waited in the van for me. I wished she'd come in, but I braved the uneven parking lot one baby step at a time.

Wow it's a good thing I have these ski poles with me! I'm so tired I can barely walk! I'm really unsteady! Ok girl, just a few more steps…

Climbing thankfully into the front passenger seat, I told Jetta she'd been right about the afternoon's testing and about being too tired to finish. I told her about the follow-up appointment as I was laying my seat back as far as it would go. I was sound asleep in almost no time.

I woke up not far from home feeling groggy and still really tired. I fought sleep the rest of the way home and remembered almost nothing about the trip. Struggling my way inside, I was almost immediately asleep in my recliner, leaving Jetta to explain the day's events to our waiting parents.

Over the next several days I realized the wisdom in the doctor's decision to wait a couple weeks to finish the testing. I was wiped out! Any conversations I had to have were brief and to the point. I stumbled over sentences or forgot altogether what the conversation was about. I couldn't concentrate on anything for more than a few minutes. My brain was completely exhausted. Just mush.

And it affected my whole body. I found that both the painful zingers and the general body fatigue were much worse. My appetite suffered too. I had no desire to go anywhere or do anything except sit and stare. I did that sometimes for hours. For several days, I felt almost like I'd had two or three chemo treatments back-to-back. It was a zombie world of pain and total exhaustion.

I came out of it slowly, and I had to let it be slow. I simply had no capacity for anything else, but day by day I gained inches of awareness. Little by little, I began to eat again. Eventually I was able to hold normal conversations and not get lost in them. I'd returned fully to my new 'normal' by a couple days before the second appointment.

Full of dread, Jetta and I went back to the testing office, but that afternoon we got a nice surprise. The testing wasn't quite as rigorous, or at least I was able to handle it slightly better this time. It lasted a little less than two hours.

Leaving the office, I climbed into the passenger seat and looked at Jetta. "Coffee? We could stop at the gas station we always stopped at with EMS."

Jetta smiled. "Well, I guess today went a little better, huh?"

"You could say that, I guess. It was still hard, and I'm tired and drained, but not nearly as bad. And coffee sounds wonderful!"

"Then coffee it is," laughed Jetta. She was greatly relieved to see me smiling and mostly alert, talking in full sentences and actually wanting to stop for coffee. She knew I would most likely still fall asleep on the way home, but oh what a difference from two weeks ago!

After that life fell into a routine again. Of course, it was another new routine. The specialist sent me to start therapy again, both PT and OT. As the results from the neuropsychologist's testing wouldn't be available for several weeks, there was really nothing more to be done. Once a month I had a blood draw and saw the oncologist and I also met with the specialist.

PT and OT were twice a week and oh did I ever dread them. Yes, the therapy helped, but at the same time it was painful, frustrating, and a little scary. I'd automatically developed a rather wide stance while walking, in order to keep as much balance as possible. Now I had to try to unlearn that habit. Yikes! It was like trying to walk the high wire without a net.

When the results from the neuropsychologist's testing finally arrived, I had to brace myself before facing those answers, and it was a good thing I did. The results report was nine pages long. It went into great detail describing how I'd fared in each segment of testing. Most of it was psychology *gobbledy-gook* to me, but Jetta found it fascinating.

I went straight to the bottom line. I found it on the second to last page under the heading 'Recommendations'. There were three small sections, and my nurse brain homed in on several phrases in them. Then I came to one little two-word phrase that stopped me cold.

Flipside

"...fully disabled..."

Two words. Just two, and I was wrong. They weren't little words. They were HUGE! I couldn't get past them. Those two words stuck in my mind when nothing else would. If I had any fight left in me, it all drained out right then. It took me a while to realize why. At first, I was just numb with shock. I couldn't process it. In fact, I couldn't deal with it at all. Once again I spent several days crying a lot, and withdrew into myself. I desperately needed to shut out this big world that had suddenly become so terrifyingly crazy.

But eventually the fog of shock receded. Eventually I was able to pray again. Eventually I sort of woke up, squared my mental shoulders, and faced it. It was only then that I began to understand why those two 'little' words had hit me so hard. It was like someone had taken a scalpel, sliced painfully through all the layers of self-protection I'd erected and peeled them back to reveal the deepest truth. A truth I'd sort of known but was trying hard to bury and keep hidden from myself.

Because those two 'little' words struck at the very core of who I thought I was. For almost thirty years now, most of my identity had been wrapped around and intertwined with my career as a nurse. I was proud of being a nurse. I was good at being a nurse. I prided myself on being a good nurse. It was a position and status symbol in my self-constructed world.

And every part of that world came crashing down around me with those two 'little' words.

What am I supposed to do with this?? What am I if I'm not a nurse? Have I truly outlived my usefulness? Is there even a point to being ME anymore? And what does 'being ME' even mean now?? Am I going to be disabled for the rest of my life? What kind of purpose is there for me in that?

The awful questions swirled around and around inside me, churning my gut along with my mind. But over the past year I'd learned a lot about handling monumental, unanswerable questions. So now, when what was left of my life was once again in a hurricane of upheaval and distress, I began to pray – a LOT.

This could not be quickly dealt with and put aside. I couldn't just face it and then move on. I didn't know where or what to move on *to*. Yes, I was making some slow physical progress. But toward *what*? I didn't know. Didn't have the faintest idea. I did, however, now know that it was going to take a long time to get there And I was going to have to just relax and let it.

I eventually reached a place of trying to accept. That acceptance came very, very slowly to me, but it steadily grew over time. I had made my decision, and it was firm. I had given myself to my Father in heaven. I knew beyond any doubt that He still loved me and was still working everything out for my good. I couldn't see the big picture. He could. So, if God now wanted to strip away my pride and the only identity I was familiar with, so be it. He could have them.

I strove every day, many times a day, to just trust Him with the rest of me.

CHAPTER TWENTY-FOUR

Two very good things happened, though.

First, I got to return to church. The COVID-19 pandemic had forced churches to find a different way of holding services, so many, ours included, had developed the use of live online services. Throughout the surgeries and chemotherapy, I had to stay home and watch the service that way. Although my faith was being fed regularly, it just wasn't the same.

At first, my return was for very short periods. Since I didn't have the stamina to make it through a whole Sunday morning, my dad or sister would come pick me up after Sunday School in time for the worship service. Then they'd hustle me back home immediately afterward so I wouldn't get swamped with people.

Gradually I got stronger. I began going on occasional short rides to the beach or for drives out in the country with Jetta. Small outings to get me out of the house and begin to build my strength a little. After a while, I felt ready for a full Sunday morning.

It was Easter Sunday. Resurrection Day! I was so excited to go celebrate my Lord's victory over death and the grave! This year it was with a far deeper appreciation than I'd ever had before.

Les, Gemma, and Ian were visiting. Les had recently gone through another cardiac stent placement and was as weak and tired as I was. He and Gemma took me to church with them, having deliberately waited to arrive after service had already started. Finding a seat at the back of the sanctuary, the three of us slid into the end of the row near the wall. Standing to sing with the congregation thrilled me. It had been so long! I desperately wanted to close my eyes as I sang, lifting my hands in worship, but that just wasn't possible. Still, holding on tightly to the back of the pew in front of me, I sang at the top of my lungs, filled with joy and thankfulness. Oh the wonder of getting to meet with God's people again to worship Him together!

During the second song I began to get tired. Side-stepping to the left a little to widen my stance in order to maintain my balance, my numb foot met resistance. I forgot that I'd put my purse down at my feet. It was too much. My weight had already begun shifting to the left foot in preparation of the wider stance. Turning quickly to look down at my feet to see what was wrong was my final undoing. My brain's inability to locate my feet, coupled with the dizzying quick turn of my head, caused balance to be a thing of the past. Down I went, falling completely to the floor on my left side.

No! Oh great. Hmmm no apparent injury – except my pride. And no doubt some new bruises. How many people saw that? Oh how embarrassing. Well, at least we're at the back of the sanctuary. And at least I wore a long dress. Hopefully I can keep a little dignity intact.

The woman I had fallen toward gasped and got Gemma's attention. Alarmed to see me on the floor, Gemma tried to help me up. They were both frightened by my fall. I was mortified.

"Are you ok? Are you hurt? What happened?" Gemma needed an explanation. I couldn't really blame her. If our places had been reversed I'd have been worried too.

After that Gemma resolutely moved to my other side, putting me between her and Les. I felt like a fool. I'd have to be a lot more careful. Sinking into a seat on the pew, I closed my eyes and prayed, resolutely giving it to my loving Father and thanking Him that no damage had been done. In the process, I happily discovered that in this position I could easily allow myself to get lost in worship.

Les, Gemma, and I snuck out just before the close of the service. Les and I were exhausted and soon resting in recliners at our parents' home. It went against the grain for both of us to have to sit and rest instead of helping prepare the meal, but neither of us had any stamina reserves left. The meal, however, was a joyous time of togetherness for all of us.

After that I went to church regularly. It pushed my limits of concentration, and always left me exhausted, but it was so wonderful to connect and worship with the family of God again!

The second good thing that happened was that I got to go back home to my own house. Temporarily.

My family felt very unsure about this move. Mostly because I was still a long, long way from being self-sufficient. I'd been living with my parents all this time, with Jetta only a mile away. But my house was almost fifteen minutes outside our little town. And yes, my neighbors were absolutely wonderful, but that wouldn't be nearly the same as having family in literally the next room.

Something in me just said it was time. And I knew it would be short-lived. I had wrestled with the decision over and over again, but I finally admitted that it was time to sell my perfect home. I simply couldn't take care of it by myself anymore. I couldn't even shovel the walk or mow the lawn. I so deeply cherished the beauty and solitude there, but I knew I'd have to find another place to get those things. Talking it over with my family, I'd decided to try to get an apartment close to them.

I broke the news to Matt and Linea that I'd decided to sell, and gave them three months to find another place to live. That was hard. I loved them both so much and I knew my house was the perfect setup for them and their dogs. I didn't want to make things hard for them.

But eventually they completed the move and I moved back in. Slowly my family and I began to clean up the house, yard, and garage. With my physical limitations and their other responsibilities, it was a long process. Especially since I was having so much trouble actually committing to putting it up for sale. This was MY place! My quiet retreat from the world. So I dragged my feet about it for months. I got the paperwork ready, had my dad fix a few things, sold some pieces of furniture, and staged the house for showing to potential buyers.

Then I stalled out.

A few months went by in much the same way. PT and OT came to an end with me working on trying to stimulate the feeling in my hands, beginning to learn to handle stairs, and practicing various balancing activities. And honestly, I felt like I was doing pretty well; handling the challenges like a pro.

Yup, pride – there it was again. I hadn't learned my lesson yet. A word to the wise: get rid of your pride! It's a sure bet it's going to trip you up.

The first time I tried to walk on the beach with Jetta, I got a nasty shock. For many years I had worn the same kind of sandals during the summer – the kind with a post between the first and second toes to help keep them on. With such completely numb feet I figured these sandals would work well. Oh how very wrong I was! We got to 'our' beach and found it delightfully deserted. I put the sandals on in the van and got out. Taking a couple of steps, I suddenly cried out in pain.

"What's wrong?" Jetta was instantly at my side.

Whimpering, I grabbed onto her arm and kicked off the sandals.

"Oh that hurt! It still hurts so bad I can hardly stand up!" Leaning on Jetta I limped my way back to the van.

"What happened? What hurts?" Jetta hovered, confused by my sudden outburst.

"As soon as I put those sandals on it felt kinda uncomfortable. I thought I was just not used to wearing sandals and had to get used to it again. But walking in them sent horrible pains shooting through my feet and up my legs! I can't wear those."

Jetta was slightly relieved, but still worried. "Are you ok? Do you need to go home?"

By then I'd recovered a bit and I jutted my chin out stubbornly. "No, I want to walk on the beach. I'll just go barefoot."

That set of my chin relaxed Jetta enough to smile. She knew that look. My stubbornness was legendary. Now Jetta was proud of me. She understood me better than anyone in the world, so she recognized what I wasn't saying: that I wasn't going to let this disease take my favorite place away from me.

It wasn't easy, though. I had extremely poor balance on firm, level ground. This was loose beach sand that constantly shifted underfoot. But I was determined.

I took one of the bagged beach chairs to use as a sturdy cane and held tightly onto Jetta's arm with the other hand. She carried the other chair and very slowly, with many stops to regain my equilibrium, we baby-stepped our way to our favorite spot.

It was right at the water's edge where a large rock was half buried in the sand. That rock was the perfect height for us to rest our feet on while looking out over the waves. I sat on the rock while Jetta set up our chairs. Then, thankfully plopping into the chairs, we both sighed in contentment. The breeze was cool off the water, but we'd come prepared. We each put on a jacket and wrapped up in a cozy blanket. For a while we talked very little.

Closing my eyes, I felt my mind and body gradually relax in the feel of the wind and the sound of the waves. This was a place like no other. Where there was never complete stillness, and yet there was immense peace. A peace in the heart, in the soul. It washed over me now in glorious waves. I soaked it in gratefully. All the effort had been well worth it.

Eventually we decided it was time to attempt a walk along the shore. That was an adventure! Again, I held tightly to Jetta's arm for support, but I still walked like a drunken sailor on the uneven ground. We laughed uproariously and kept walking.

We'd learned this skill over the past several months; to laugh instead of cry with the challenges. And really it was funny. If anybody had been watching they'd no doubt have thought the worst. Oh well. At one point I made the mistake of deciding to get my feet wet in the clear, shimmering water. Mistake. Big time mistake. The water was cold. It felt like knives in my feet and sent painful shocks up through my legs.

Trying to get past the pain, I sighed heavily. "Do you think I'll ever be able to go swimming again? I love the water."

"Yes," Jetta answered firmly. Then she laughed. "I was going to say you just have to be patient. Then I remembered that's SO not your strong suit."

Laughing too, I shot back, "Hey, everybody's got their weak points!"

We walked for several minutes, talking through much that had happened in the past year. How everything had so dramatically changed.

That day we discovered an amazing, seemingly impossible joy. As shocking, awful, horrible, painful, sickening, depressing, and fearful as this whole cancer journey had been, it had brought about a depth of closeness – with each other and with God – that blew us away. That closeness had been realized by each member of our family. We'd definitely 'circled the wagons' at the beginning, but the far-reaching results of that instinctive reaction were still being realized. We marveled together at how frequent and fervent our prayers had become. How our family had developed a rich, daily connection through group texting that had never been there before. Almost every day now members of the family were posing and discussing questions and highlights we'd come across in our Bible reading, just to share the marvels of God with each other.

Jetta and I had grown closer too. That sounds so minimal to say, and doesn't even begin to describe our fantastic relationship. The two of us had become very close while in high school. Though sisters, we were also best friends. Over the years of not living near each other, that closeness had dwindled, but never really died. Now, however, having gone through battle after battle side by side throughout the past year, we shared a connection that was awesome. I never use that word lightly. I find few things other than God Himself to be truly worthy of awe. But this bond was directly from that same God, so how could it be less? Walking unsteadily along the beach that day, we laughed and cried with pure JOY in the delight of this bond we shared. In all the awfulness, it was a gift, a rare gem that we both knew would now last forever.

We'd really only gone a short distance, though, when I had to stop.

"I'm sorry. We better turn back now or I'm gonna be too exhausted to make it."

"No apologies!" Jetta turned slowly around with me, supporting me carefully. "I'm actually surprised at how far we've come. You made it farther than I expected."

The wind had picked up during our short walk and it was turning colder. Jetta's close friend Ann met us on our way back. She took my other arm, but she was too short to be much help that way. I laughed and threw my arm around Ann's shoulders. We all trooped happily back together.

That August my daughter Jamie and her boyfriend Henry came to visit. Since they lived all the way across the country in Oregon, I'd never met him. I loved him immediately. Jamie had, of course, told me a lot about him, but now I got to enjoy getting to know him a bit myself. I often smiled privately to myself during that visit, wondering when they'd decide to get married. If I had to bet, I'd say they wouldn't be waiting very long. Maybe I'd soon get the excitement of helping plan their wedding!

CHAPTER TWENTY-FIVE

I finally closed on the sale of my beloved house in the middle of March. It was then just over one year since my final chemo treatment. I moved back in with my parents and settled down to wait. My name was on the waiting list for a one-bedroom apartment in our little town.

Almost immediately after I sold the house, a bunch of us traveled to Florida. For the first time in my life, I visited some of the Disney World parks. That was such a fun trip! We stayed in a multi-level condo-type resort (that thankfully had elevators) with lovely palm trees, walking paths, and swimming pools. Since my brother Les and I were both having troubles, we took a wheelchair with us. It got a lot of use in the huge parks. Leaving the cold northern Michigan winter to soak up some warm Florida sunshine was a dream come true.

But the one-year mark came and went and not much had changed. I was still having the same concentration problems. My short-term memory was full of holes, and I often completely forgot conversations or events that happened just yesterday. The painful 'zingers' were still happening all the time. The numbness had thankfully receded from most of my torso, but still fully engulfed my arms and legs. So my balance was still very bad.

A whole year! And yes, my body has improved, but only very slightly. My brain hasn't improved at all. Is my central nervous system irreparably damaged? Am I going to be this limited for the rest of my life?!

Six months after I'd applied for federal social security benefits, I'd been approved. I began receiving a monthly check. Somehow, I was also still approved for ongoing long-term disability benefits through work. I received a monthly check from them too. The low amounts scared me at first, though. I was so used to the professional wage I'd received for so many years as an experienced nurse.

As it turned out, there were no apartments available in our little town in northern Michigan, and the waiting list was long. One day I was sitting at the table playing Aggravation with Mom when I got a text from Gemma.

"Since there are no apartments up there, have you considered the possibility of moving down here? There are lots of apartments available near us."

I hadn't, but the idea appealed to me. It would be a brand-new start in a brand-new place. I'd still have family nearby, and the winters would be milder.

"Hmmm that's a good question. I'll have to think about it. Can you check into some places for me? I'd need a one-bedroom apartment on the ground floor. And it would have to be barrier-free because of my balance problems."

Gemma was excited about this possibility and began the search. And that's how it happened. Just over one year out from the end of chemo I moved three hours downstate. My new apartment was all I'd asked for and more. Small and simple, it was on the ground floor, barrier-free, and included a sliding glass door with a small cement patio. It looked out over a large lawn area with, about fifty yards away, several individual garden plots that tenants could use during the summer.

I loved it immediately. It meant getting back a large measure of the independence I'd had to give up over the past year. And privacy! Complete, nearly silent privacy! Oh how I treasured the silence.

Unfortunately, it also meant being far away from the loved ones who'd supported me unwaveringly throughout the darkest days of my life. It was wrenching to have to leave Jetta, my parents, and Dana, not to mention Matt and his family. It broke my heart even through the excitement of moving to a new place. It felt like the first book was ending so a sequel could start.

As I settled into my new home, it felt really strange to be so alone again. And disconnected. Up north I'd known a lot of people in the community and had been active in a close-knit ladies' Bible study at church. If not for Les, Gemma, and Ian, I'd have drowned in loneliness and depression (Of course, if they hadn't been there I'd never have moved there in the first place.) But they immediately wove me into the fabric of their daily lives. My apartment being only about 6 minutes from their home helped immensely.

I started going to church with them. It was a bigger church than I was used to, so it took some time to get comfortable there. Les and I had known the pastor in college, and I came to love his preaching style. As Les put it, it was "like you were sitting with him over a good cup of coffee and just talking together." After a few weeks some of the faces were familiar and I began to enjoy it more.

Henry and Jamie got married that summer. In typical Jamie fashion, there were two weddings. The first was in Oregon in April. I flew out there with the help of my ex-husband, Jamie's dad. It was a simple, but beautiful wedding outdoors on a covered bridge, with blossoming apple trees just across the way. The second wedding was also very beautiful; in June, in Michigan, in a tiny country chapel with wildflowers in bloom all around. Both were small, intimate gatherings. What a wonderful privilege it was to welcome a new son into our family!

A few months later Henry and Jamie moved across the country to Michigan. They got an apartment just three minutes from mine. Oh my happy heart! Now all my kids were nearby as Jude lived with his dad only an hour away.

EPILOGUE

And so, the next chapter of life begins. And life is good!

Jude only has one year of graduate school left, so I'm trying to soak up as much time with him as possible. He comes up to stay with me as often as we can work it out.

I'm having fun getting to know my new son-in-law, Henry. He's fun and witty and the perfect match for Jamie. They just found out they're expecting my first grandchild in early February. I'm so excited!

I can drive short distances, so I'm able to do my own grocery shopping, though it really tires me out. Ian, who I dubbed 'My Guy' at birth, has become my walker. Most places we go, we go all together, so he lets me hold his arm for stability. I still walk funny with a kind of wide stance. And curbs and stairs are awful things in my world. But usually Ian is there and ready to help me. He's only fifteen, but is already 6 feet 2 inches tall. He's my steady rock to lean on.

At the advice of the specialist, I've gotten a membership at our local athletic club so I can join in the aquatic exercise classes. Oooohhhh the relief of being in the heated pool! As soon as I'm down the steps and truly in the water, my poor, anxious brain just seems to go AAAAHHHHHH!! No more fear of falling. The water's buoyancy frees my brain from all its constant stress. And the exercises in the water are no-impact, so my neuropathy pain isn't triggered so badly. I go almost every day and love it every time. Of course, getting out of the pool is no picnic. By then my body is tired and my brain has to switch back on and work overtime to compensate. I come home from the pool exhausted, but happy.

I'm still living in that same little apartment. I'm still attending that same church with my family. I'm still on disability. Most of my body has feeling now; all but my hands, lower legs, and feet, and the numbness comes and goes in my hands. The painful zingers aren't nearly as prevalent anymore, but the neuropathy pain has ramped up to take their place. I still have very poor short-term memory and very limited concentration. My balance is still not good; I still feel like I'm going to fall nearly all the time. I'm aware that I am not safe driving long distances. It's a three-hour trip to my up-north family and friends – and doctors. That's way too long for me to try to concentrate. So, my family meets halfway and hands me off, much like divorced parents giving their kids back and forth.

Who am I now? What am I now? That's hard to say. Officially, I'm in remission. Some say I kicked cancer's butt. Utter nonsense! If there was any butt-kicking, I was definitely on the receiving end.

Some call me a Survivor. It's hard to explain why I'm uncomfortable with that title. Maybe it's because I don't feel it's been earned. Yes, as of right at this moment, I'm confident that I'm cancer-free. Well, mostly confident. The statistics for recurrence of my type of cancer are quite high. And the huge fear of it coming back hits me out of the blue. No warning. All of a sudden, I'll be swamped in extreme anxiety, just sure it's lurking in my body waiting to be found. Having talked with many cancer patients, I've learned this fear is now a fact of life. It's apparently not unusual that I second- and third-guess every minute change in my body, monitoring every little bump and sniffle and pain to the nth degree,

In her book, *Healing: When A Nurse Becomes A Patient*, Theresa Brown, RN, describes this very problem:

"...no one talks about an absolute end-point to having the disease. Cancer patients are generally denied the decisiveness of a 'cure'. ... Having no disease was good, but cured? One hundred percent cured? As in, like measles or mumps, that person could never get cancer again? No. Doesn't happen. No guarantees, no promises. That is why, sometimes, I suddenly feel the fear."

In another place in the same book, she makes the statement, "'I had cancer' feels nothing like 'I have cancer'." How profound! And so painfully true. Yes, some days I'm strong enough to say the words "I had cancer." But the difficulty in saying those three words is not even in the same galaxy as the soul-deep agony of having to admit it in the present tense.

I had to make that admission once. I don't ever want to again.

Regardless of the future, I now know what cancer patients mean by, "It's a good day today," versus, "I'm having a bad day today." I think probably anyone with a chronic or long disease process gets this. I can't adequately describe it, so I won't try. All I'll say is that there are days I can handle facing this new life with all its craziness, and there are days I can't. And I do mean can't. Total shutdown is real. There are degrees to this, of course. Most days are somewhere in the middle.

BUT GOD...!!!

I've saved the best part for last.

There are those who would shrug off this part of my story, dismissing it as a trite convenience that I sought for and found what I decided to call 'God' in the panicked distress of a life-threatening disease. To those cynics I say, "SHAME on you!" I'm calling you out. You've been inattentive. Did I not say at the beginning that I had already spent some three years as a renewed, growing Christian before my tumor was ever found?

This is by far the most personal part for me. The deepest part. Now, after all these long months of trial, I do truly know beyond a shadow of a doubt that God is directly and intimately involved in every tiny detail of our lives. I've seen Him in action time and time again. There is a deep wonder to life. A richness that can't be denied.

A peace that cannot be fathomed by human understanding.

Most people are looking for something. I know I was. I desired money, possessions and the freedom to do whatever I wanted to do whenever I wanted to do it. And I prided myself in my knowledge and position as an experienced nurse. For many years I worked as a professional and earned a professional wage, and maybe someday I will again. I don't know. What I do know is that in all those years nothing was enough.

You often see it as comedy now – a parent dropping their child off at school or somewhere, and as the child is walking away, the parent calls out, "Make good choices!" It's not funny. I know from personal experience. Poor choices hurt. And they cause a lot of regrets and emptiness. I tried a lot of things: relationships and sex, alcohol to have fun, buying whatever I wanted on a whim, some exotic traveling. And never in all that time did I feel like I'd arrived. Like I'd finally gotten to where I'd always wanted to be or gotten all I wanted to get. Not once.

And now?

I have significant physical and mental limitations. I need help with simple tasks I once had the luxury of taking for granted. Things like cooking a meal on the stove and chopping up vegetables and stepping up or down at a curb. I live on a set, limited income. I've had to learn a level of dependence I would very recently have been horrified to even consider.

And yet, I am more serenely content than almost anyone I know.

I'm still a very flawed person. I still need reminding and correcting. I still hurt people sometimes. I still do thoughtless, inconsiderate things and let words come out of my mouth that I wish I could take back. And yes, I'm still plagued by fears of the future.

I realize I sound like I'm contradicting myself. And maybe you have to experience this amazing peace for yourself in order to understand. But here's the long and the short of it: fear has nothing to hold on to when that peace comes in. Not even a toe-hold. And that peace comes from love. Love so complete, so indescribably strong, so filled with empathetic compassion that it rules all. How do I know this peace comes from love? Personal experience aside, it says in 1 John 4:18, "Perfect love drives out fear." Ever read 'the love chapter' of the Bible? It's 1 Corinthians 13. That's a definition of love to challenge all others. Especially verses 4 through 8a.

Perfect love. Perfect. There for the asking. No hoops to jump through. No stack of papers to sign. No empty handshake that's easily forgotten. Just an acknowledgment that I've done wrong and need Someone's help. Just a request for forgiveness from the only true GOD. That's it. The recipe for peace.

Too simple? Too childish? When was the last time you followed 'I'm sorry' with 'Will you please forgive me?' It's not exactly easy. It's extremely humbling. But it's powerful even among people we love. It's exponentially more powerful when you say it to God and mean it. That's where the peace comes from.

So no, I'm not contradicting myself. I'm learning – finally – what really LIVING means. And I'm having the time of my life here on the flipside.

This is where I get to say, "But God…" Because He makes all the difference.

ABOUT THE AUTHOR

In this debut autobiographical work, author Leeann Jordan dares to lead her readers through the trials of her journey through cancer and ongoing recovery. With almost thirty years of experience in the medical field, including many different positions as a Registered Nurse, EMT, and instructor for Medical Terminology, CPR, and nurse aide training classes, her life was flipped upside down when she was forced to experience the medical world as a patient instead. Leeann resides near her family in central Michigan, and enjoys gardening, spending time with her two adult children, and learning to thrive after the chaos.

Made in the USA
Middletown, DE
15 October 2023

40810527R00124